Ani-La
the nuns from Redna Menling

Sidestone Press

Ani-La
the nuns from Redna Menling

Joke van de Belt

© 2010 J. van de Belt

Published by Sidestone Press, Leiden
www.sidestone.com
Sidestone registration number: SSP58010001

ISBN 978-90-8890-046-4

Translation: Evert van Tijn

Photographs cover: Tibetan prayer flags
Cover design: K. Wentink, Sidestone Press
Lay-out: P.C. van Woerdekom, Sidestone Press

Contents

Acknowledgement   7

The use of Tibetan terminology   8

Summary   9

1 Preamble | the Nuns of Redna Menling   **11**
   1.1 Preamble   11
   1.2 Problem Area   12
      1.2.1 The Tibetan History of the Bon   12
      1.2.2 Bon and Buddhism   13
      1.2.3 Scholarly Research into the Bon   15
      1.2.4 Scholarly Research into Nuns and Women in the Bon   17
   1.3 Objective of Research   19
   1.4 Research Questions   20
   1.5 Methods and my Role as a Scholarly Researcher   20

2 The Bon | A Community in Exile   **23**
   2.1 Introduction   23
   2.2 The Bon Community in Dolanji   23
      2.2.1 The Community of Nuns in Dolanji   30
   2.3 The Set-up of the Project   32
      2.3.1 Observations   33
      2.3.2 Interviews with Nuns and with Informants   35
   2.4 The group in Research   36
      2.4.1 Composition, Backgrounds and Daily Life   36

3 Reasons to profess | What makes a young woman become a nun?   **43**
   3.1 Introduction   43
   3.2 Personal and Social Background in the Country of Origin   44
   3.3 Connections between Biography and Motives to Profess   47
      3.3.1 Practical Considerations   48
      3.3.2 Inspired by Religion   49
      Portrait of Ani Kunsel Wangmo   *50*
      3.3.3 A Choice Forced by Political Reality   51
      Portrait of Ani Monlam Sangmo   *52*
      Portrait of Ani Yangzo Dolmo   *54*
   3.4 The Ties between Daily Life and the Expectations of Life as a Nun   55
      3.4.1 Theoretical Intermezzo: Communitas   62

4 The community of nuns | Interaction with its surroundings   **65**
  4.1 Religious Praxis and Integration in Daily Life   65
    4.1.1 The Aim of Religious Praxis   65
    4.1.2 Gender, the Body and the Religious Praxis   69
    4.1.3 Theoretical Intermezzo: Gender and the Physical Body   74
    4.1.4 The Impact of the Research   77

5 Conclusion | The Nuns of Redna Menling   **79**
  5.1 Introduction   79
  5.2 Macro Level: The Nuns Place inside the Bon   80
  5.3 Meso Level: Reasons to Profess and Life in a Monastic Community   81
  5.4 Gender, Celibacy and Ritual Praxis   83
  5.5 Epilogue   85

Appendix 1: Glossary   *87*

Appendix 2: Letter   *89*

Bibliography   *91*

Acknowledgement

For Carla
Because boundaries are not always found to be boundaries

It was in Wettingen, a village close to Zurich, that on Friday 12th of July 2008 I sat and watched a staging of Faust's *Goethe*. In this version Faust in desperation swings the door of his study wide open to cast his books out of the window, shouting: 'Philosophy, mathematics, theology [or maybe religion, that's even to me] do not bring me any answers!'

In that scene Faust fairly accurately sums up the feelings that haunted me then, even though I have not, I sincerely hope, sold my soul to the devil in exchange for fitting answers. But the doubts he expressed uncomfortably resembled mine, as I experienced in the midst of the process of writing my thesis about the Nuns of Redna Menling.

The thesis was the result of four intensive, thrilling, interesting years, during which I certainly was overcome by doubt at whiles. Four years of study, fieldwork in India, culminating in a thesis, I really couldn't have done it without the help and support of a great number of others. Without them the curiosity and the dreams, which guided me back to the classroom, probably would have ended in despondency.

First of all I want to thank Joseph, my 'lief'. His support, his care, his love and his belief in my qualities made sure that I could live this dream. For four long years he spent a considerable part of our communal life alone, as I went to class in Holland or was doing fieldwork in India. Time and again he eased my doubts and uncertainties, and every time I was ready to quit he was there to restore my courage and confidence. Darling ,'lief', thank you.

My thanks go to Claudia, an unbelievable precious friend, beyond all borders and time zones, who was always there to lift me up, to save me from silly steps, and conjured up one of her indispensable bits of humour, whenever I needed it.

My sisters Ietje and Cobie were there at every test I took and passed, cheering and yelling as if the Swiss football team had won the World Championship. That is a dream, as we all know, but dreams is what we need and dreams should be kept alive so that in the end they can be made true. That is what the two of you did, by believing that I could do it. Thank you.

Special thanks go to His Holiness Lungtok Tenpai Nyima, 33rd Menri Trinzin, spiritual leader of the Bon. Without his support my research and fieldwork couldn't have taken place. The openness and willingness with which the community of Dolanji embraced my work were made possible by the way His Holiness introduced me. What is more, his care and dedication created a second 'home' for me.

Much I owe to the Lopan, headmaster of the school for Geshes of the Menri Monastery. He lent me his support in the search for history and for the place nuns hold of old in the Bon. Both his enthusiasm and the amount of time he made available proved to be of immeasurable value.

I want to thank all the Geshes who were willing to meet me and to give their insights on the place and position of the nuns. Thank you very much. But special gratitude I feel for Geshe Sonam, who took care of me and never failed to answer my many questions.

Thanks for Tasho Tomo, who didn't only took care of all the translations and interpreting, but who also became a good friend and invited me in into her family, providing me with a real home, those three months in Dolanji.

Prof.dr. Eric Venbrux has earned my distinctive appreciation for his enthusiasm, his proficient coaching and his encouraging words, both during the fieldwork and while writing. His support helped me to master the many obstacles and gather the best in me, time after time.

I end with words of thank to Tsering, Yangzo, Tsering, Monlam, Rinchen, Tender, Tswang, Metok, Sherap, Tashi, Tsundu, Monlam, Kunsel, Namdak, Lobsang, Kunsang, Samten, Tsultim, 'my' Anis. Words cannot express my feelings of thankfulness. Your readiness to talk with me, to welcome me in the community of the monastery, to share with me your tales and dreams was a gift beyond expectation. Without the stories and dreams of the Nuns of Redna Menling there wouldn't have been any research and I would not have been able to write my thesis or this book.

Joke van de Belt
October 2008/January 2010

The use of Tibetan terminology

The use of Tibetan words and terminology in this thesis calls for clarification.

The Tibetan language is based on Sanskrit and has its own writing. As I do not speak or read the language myself, I had to rely on others. I decided to use the phonetic transcription of Geshe Sonam. With his help the most commonly used words were translated and transcribed.

Summary

Research on the place of nuns in the Bon religion really is pioneering work. There is hardly any research available and in the studies that can be found the adopted approach is biased. That is why I have chosen for fieldwork (interviews and participating observation) in Redna Menling, the nunnery of the Menri Monastery in Dolanji – India.

I made the stories of the nuns my starting point. Supplementing these narratives with information from interviews and conversations with informants from the wider community, field observations and a theoretical orientation, I succeeded to extract from this micro level study insights into the status of nuns in the community in exile (meso level) and in the Bon religion as a whole (macro level).

Chapter 1 informs about the role and origin of the Bon religion in Tibet and its relationship to Buddhism. It is a complex history, which reveals a certain analogy with regard to organization and belief system between Bon and Buddhism. But it also shows that the Bon has succeeded to uphold itself as an independent religion. Historic sources say that Tonpa Sherab, the mythical founder of the Bon, is believed to have explicitly attributed to women an equal role. This, however, seems contrary to the invisibility of nuns in the modern Bon tradition in exile.

Chapter 2 focuses specifically on the developments of the Bon in exile, the explicit context in which the nuns of Redna Menling live and shape their monastic tradition. In Chapter 3 and 4 the nuns speak for themselves. However diverse the motives of the individual women to enter the convent of Redna Menling, they can be divided into three main categories: 1) Practical considerations, such as the possibility to study, 2) Religiously inspired, 3) Political and economic conditions in the Nepalese uplands (where most women come from). But however different their motives, together they constitute the first female monastic Bon community in exile.

Although the religious praxis cannot be fully practised, due to a lack of experience and the level of education, learning and practicing some of the religious praxis are the binding elements in the nuns' community. Characteristic of this community is liminality and within this liminality a social structure develops that acquires a permanent character.

In their vows these women see celibacy as a main topic. Physicality and control over the body is a recurring theme in the lives of the nuns of Redna Menling. This is consistent with the theory of Mary Douglas in *Natural Symbols*, which states that the amount of structure and control a society exercises is reflected in the way control is exerted over the body (Douglas, 1996). The nuns depend in many respects on the men's monastery and this dependence creates a sharp awareness of what is lawful and what is not. By controlling the body (refrain from sexual activities and make sure not to offend) the women show they are good nuns and novices.

The convent is a new phenomenon in the religious community of Dolanji and it necessarily attracts attention both inside and outside the community. This increases the pressure to strictly follow the written and unwritten rules. The impact of globalization in the form of fund raising and financial support from Europe and America, conveying Western ideas about for instance gender relations towards Dolanji, leave their mark on the community.

With this exploratory research, I have opened a new direction in research into women in the Bon. I wish to give an impetus for further investigation. Multidisciplinary research is needed to fully define and understand the place of the female monastic tradition and the position of (individual) nuns.

Chapter 1

Preamble | the Nuns of Redna Menling

1.1 Preamble

"No, but we are different. Tonpa Sherab treated men and women in the same way, he passed on his teachings to both men and women and that is why with us nuns enjoy the same position as monks, quite unlike the Buddhists."

That is the standard reaction I was given for the past ten years, when probing the position of nuns in the Bon. Questions about the virtual invisibility of women in the monastic tradition were usually answered like this: "Oh yes, that is our culture."

Some fifteen years ago a series of chance meetings brought me in contact with the Bon tradition, a religion rooted in Tibet and claiming to be the original Tibetan religion.

In the beginning I could not keep apart Buddhism and the Bon. Only after an intensive meeting with Geshe* Nyima Dakpa, in the summer of 1999, it slowly began to dawn on me that in spite of the many similarities they are two distinct religions. I discovered the two are different in history, in symbolic systems, in customs and in rituals. I was spellbound and in the years that followed I became a regular visitor of the Menri Monastery of the Bon in India.

What struck me was the absence of nuns in the monastic tradition at Menri. Indeed, there were some nuns but they did not take part in monastic life. These women took their vows at a ripe age after leaving traditional family life. In 2004 a shift took place. All of a sudden, to my eyes at least, I noticed a number of mainly young women who had made their vows and presented themselves as novices. At the same time the construction of a nunnery started, the first convent of the Bon in exile.

I was fascinated, but this development also fuelled a number of questions: Who are these young women? Where do they come from? Why do young women, living in modern times, choose to lead a life that is marked by practising spirituality? Why do they choose for tight rules and rhythms, for a life dedicated to contemplation and long studies in a more or less isolated position? I could not help thinking that as for equality nuns in this monastic tradition have a long way to go, however many times I was comforted that in the Bon tradition nuns and monks have equal opportunities of schooling and progress.

These observations and my personal fascination for the place and position of women in an age-old tradition, sculptured the rough outlines of a subject for my master studies and its thesis.

1.2 Problem Area

Tibet is the land of everlasting snow, the land of holy men and a stray holy woman, vast steppes with the coloured accents of waving prayer flags and a never-ending number of monasteries. Tibet is associated with the image of holiness. Through the ages the Bon and Buddhism have tinted Tibet with a religious shade and the two are linked together irreversibly. Insight in the Bon and its development in Tibet and in the position of nuns in its monastic system requires a brief outline of the position of the Bon in Tibet, its relation with Tibetan Buddhism and the position of nuns.

The history of the Bon is confined by tradition, by the writings of Buddhist historiographers, but also by the findings of scholarly researchers. This has led to an image that though at least disputable still dominates present day research into the Bon. That is why a rather elaborate passage about the history of the Bon and the position of nuns in its monastic system is inevitable.

1.2.1 The Tibetan History of the Bon

The myth recounting the founding of the Bon tells that it is eighteen thousand years ago that Tonpa Sherab was born in the mythical celestial empire of Olmo Lung Ring. Tonpa Sherab is regarded the founder of the Bon religion. He enters his world as an enlightened being, but chooses to descend to the realm of man, where he is born the son of a king. From Olmo Lung Ring, also known by the name of Tazik or 'The Holy Land' the Bon religion spread to Zhang Zhung. Of old this kingdom was found in the western regions of Tibet, and the holy mountain Kailas was its centre. While travelling from Zhang Zhung to Tibet Tonpa Sherabs horses were stolen by a demon. On arriving in Tibet Tonpa Sherab stumbles upon a religion that practices the sacrifice of living beings. His teachings, rituals and ceremonies however succeed in stemming the spirits that spread sickness and decay, without the sacrifice of any living creature. The new religion is accepted in Tibet (Dakpa 2005, 13).

This genesis laid the foundation for what we now call Yung Drung Bon*, 'the eternal Bon'. Though the Bon and Yung Drung Bon are frequently mentioned in Tibetan history, there is much uncertainty about the way the religion has actually developed. In the oldest manuscripts available the Bon is linked to legends about gods who are regarded as guardians of the ruling kings. Scrolls found in the caves of Dunhuang in 1950 mention a group or a class of priests known by the name of Bonpo*. The manuscripts describe Tibet as it was until the seventh century, the period in which a national dynasty begins to take shape. A class of priests, designated as Bonpo, holds an important position in the burial rites of kings who even after death play a decisive role in safeguarding the country.

The Dunhuang-scrolls mention the Bod as the authentic religion of Tibet. Its counterpart is called Chos. Chos refers to what has come from outside Tibet (e.g. India and China). The Bon itself claims that it represents Tibetan religious life until the advent of Indian Buddhism (Kvaerne 1972, 27)

From its own historical perspective the Bon has to make way for the 'untrue religion' by the beginning of the 8th century after losing the protection of the king. Through a system of family lineage, however, the religion an its traditions, were kept alive to make a full recovery after a number of generations. But the Bon never regained the support of the king. (kvaerne 1995, 13)

1.2.2 Bon and Buddhism

History indicates two possible periods for the introduction of Indian Buddhism in Tibet. It is important to realise that Buddhism was already known in Tibet before its official establishment. After all Buddhism was influential in neighbouring countries such as India and China and because a slow process, influenced by a number of factors, preceded the introduction.

Around 600 CE the king of a united Tibet officially introduces Buddhism. Legend has it that he married a Chinese princess, mainly to secure the economic interests of the country. King Songten Gampo sends envoys to India. They return with Buddhist scriptures and information. Indian Buddhism is allowed to grow, even if the king himself remains dedicated to the Bon (Lowenstein 2002, 127).

In the period from approximately 700 to 1000 CE Tibet lived through turbulent times. The country rose to power, but also has very powerful neighbours to the North and East: China and Mongolia. Tibet looses its stability in a feudal strife over ownership and allocation of land. The loss of power leaves the country vulnerable to foreign raiders. The clash of interests coincides with religious troubles. The Bon is forbidden as the ruling nobility turns to Buddhism. By the end of the 8th century CE the first Buddhist monks take their vows (Baumer 1999, 16).

The Bon regains the religious upper hand in the 9th century. Buddhism is pushed out of central Tibet. The king supports the Bon, but his death triggers a civil war with different clans fighting for power. The lack of unity makes Tibet once more vulnerable as foreign bands raid the country. Tibet looses a considerable part of its territory. The absence of a centre of power rekindles the religious strife, mainly initiated by the Buddhist faction. The Bon tries to make itself known, but lacks support among the Tibetan nobility.

In the period between 1100 and 1400 a series of events in India is instrumental in shaping the religious destiny of Tibet. Islamic invaders overrun India's Northern regions. Many Buddhist monasteries and libraries are looted and destroyed. A great number of Buddhist monks flee to Tibet. Their arrival boosts the Buddhist community and sets off the development of what we know today to be Tibetan Buddhism. In due time four different Tibetan Buddhist schools evolved, each one with its own monastic tradition.

The Bon does not fade away, however. The teachings are passed on through family lines in a way that until today shapes the tradition. And by the end of the 11th century a monastic practice starts to form along Buddhist lines. The Bon more or less reorganises itself. It broadens its canon with concepts like karma* and reincarnation, but it retains its original cosmological foundation, views and rituals (Karmay 2007, 56-57).

The political and economic situation in Tibet remains tense, especially when by the end of the 14th century Mongol tribes are about to invade the country. The Gelupa Order, the 4th and also youngest school of Tibetan Buddhism, sides both politically and religiously with the Mongols. In 1656 the Mongols sustain the inauguration of the 5th Dalai Lama as the Priest-King of Tibet (Lowenstein 2002, 131). The Bon and its followers appear to remain outside the political arena, in spite of close relations between the 5th Dalai Lama and the leading clergy of the Bon. The absence of political ambition seems to be the reason that the Bon is more or less ignored (Karmay 2007, 77). But in the struggle for temporal and spiritual power, monasteries of rivalling spiritual schools are attacked and especially the Bon monasteries are targeted for looting and destruction.

The union with the Mongols was a thorn in the side of China and when under the reign of the 6th Dalai Lama chaos prevails, the Regent turns to China for help. In 1721 political power is transferred to China. Tibet and its ruling party remain responsible for internal affairs, including religion, but foreign affairs are to be a Chinese matter. Also a number of important provinces are annexed by China. Noteworthy is that most of these are provinces with prominent centres of the Bon, such as the province of Amdo.

Neighbouring Nepal decides on a treaty with Great Britain in the 18th century. In 1841 and 1855 Tibet is faced with invading Nepalese military forces. China is troubled with internal unrest and is unable to send aid. The Tibetan leadership fearing that England plans to conquer the country hermetically seals the borders. This isolation provokes a build up of tension between England and Russia. When England decides to invade Tibet the Dalai Lama flees to Mongolia and eventually settles in exile in China. In the aftermath England, Russia and China come to an agreement. Tibet and the Tibetan leaders are not to take part in the consultations. The outcome is that China gains authority over Tibet.

In 1913 the Dalai Lama declares Tibetan independence, but the new state does receive neither international support nor recognition. The future of Tibet is decided upon at the Simla Conference. The outcome is a division between an inner and an outer Tibet and China is allowed a large say in Tibetan affairs.

When in 1933 the 13th Dalai Lama dies the usual search for his incarnation starts. Two years later he is found, but the new Dalai Lama is far too young to exert any power or political influence. Again a political vacuum arises (McKay 2003-II, 1-30).

China occupies Tibet in 1959. It is the start of a dark period during which many Tibetans, both Buddhist and Bonpo flee the country into exile. Those who are forced to stay have to face repression and food shortages. Many die (McKay 2003-III, 1-32).

Among the exiles, mainly fleeing to India, are the spiritual leaders of Bon and Buddhism. The Dalai Lama decides in 1961 to set up a Tibetan parliament in exile in India. In 1977 the Bon is allotted a seat in parliament, heralding a new era in the history of Bon and Buddhism. Both face the task to reorganise and formulate a new profile in exile.

1.2.3 Scholarly Research into the Bon

Tibetan history learns that during the last centuries the Bon explicitly stayed in the background. Buddhism colours the image. This has also affected the images of the Bon that have formed. In both popular and scholarly publications, catering for the vast Western interest in Tibet and its mysterious past, the Bon is portrayed as a religion that has highly adapted to Buddhism. A good example is the popular book The Way of the White Clouds by Lama* Anagarika Govinda. Govinda recounts of his travels to several sacred places of Buddhism. During these travels he also visited a Bon monastery:

> "As only the Bonpo circumambulate anticlockwise or pass a shrine or a sacred place (like Mount Kailas) with the left shoulder turned towards it, this confirmed our notion that this was not a Buddhist abbot but a Bonpo. When entering the main temple, our last doubts vanished, for everything we saw there seemed to be a reversal or contortion of Buddhist tradition. The legs of the swastika of the Bonpo, for instance, pointed to the left, while those of the Buddhists pointed to the right. Moreover the Bonpo have copied almost every characteristic of Buddhist iconography. They have their own Buddhas and Bodhisattvas*, their own fierce guardians and gods of heaven and earth. The names may differ but for the rest they hardly differ from the originals. The same might be said of the Bon texts, which are more of less an imitation of Buddhist texts and sometimes even bear the same names. But they are attributed to other authors, take place in different surroundings and often use other mantras." (Govinda 1985, 2038-239).

This view, the Bon as a duplicate of Buddhism, though sporting a dark lining, has long dominated to image of the Bon.

In recent decennia a number of scholars has engaged in research into the Bon. Four of them, who have been op primary importance for the research into the Bon I present explicitly.

Hoffmann

The first to mention is Helmut Hoffmann, whose views have long been decisive for the reputation of the Bon. Hoffmann, professor of Ideology at the University of Munich, was the first scholar to start systematic research into the Bon. In 1950 he published his book 'Quellen zur Geschichte der Tibetischen Bon-religion' (Sources of the History of the Tibetan Bon Religion), (Hoffmann 1950). For his work he relied mainly on Buddhist sources and scriptures. This led him to the view that the Bon can be seen as a Tibetan form of shamanism that has much in common with types of shamanism found in North and Central Asia.

From this shamanism the Bon is thought to have evolved gradually toward a fusion and an integration with Buddhism, initially through tantric* movements. A number of the Bon characteristics however are mainly found in the rituals, according to Hoffmann.

This viewpoint has deeply influenced later research that in general continued in the direction set out by Hoffmann. The choice for Buddhist sources and manuscripts ensures that the Bon is regarded and considered as a religion that in order to survive has incorporated the doctrines and spiritual practices of Buddhism. It therefore may be regarded as a duplicate of Buddhism

Snellgrove

David Snellgrove retired in 1983 as professor of Tibetan Studies at the *School for Oriental and African Studies* of London University but is still active there. He was the first to take a fresh viewpoint in researching the relations between the Bon and Buddhism. Snellgrove came into contact with the Bon in 1956 during a seven months journey through remote regions of Tibet and Nepal [Dolpo and Tarap]. The outcome of these travels he laid down in '*Himalayan Pilgrimage*'. He mentions a meeting with a Bonpo Lama and his texts (Snellgrove 1961). At first Snellgrove is sceptical about the texts, but after a closer look he starts to doubt the notion that they are merely copies.

In 1961 Snellgrove invites several Bonpo monks to work with him in London on a translation of the Kanju*, 'the nine ways of the Bon'. In the introduction of the book '*The Nine Way of the Bon*' Snellgrove writes:

> "It would be naive to expect Bonpo literature to be totally different from Buddhist literature. On the contrary, it is rather remarkable that Bonpo texts contain so much comprehensible pre-Buddhist material, and it is not surprising that Bonpo composers of text (even perhaps as early as the eight or ninth century) were already entertain of the meanings of many names and terms of the indigenous (entirely oral) tradition" (Snellgrove 1967, 21).

With this quote Snellgrove in fact defines the Bon as an independent religion, opening the way to a new scholarly era. This meant that in the early seventies more and more researchers came to treat the Bon as a separate religion. The Bon becomes a subject of research in its own right.

Kvaerne

In the introduction to his book '*The Bon Religion of Tibet*' Per Kvaerne, professor in the History of Religion of Tibet at the University of Oslo comes to the following conclusion:

> "In view of the many manifest similarities between Bon and Buddhism, one may well ask in what the distinction between the two religions consists. The answer, at least to this author, would seem to depend on which perspective is adopted when describing Bon. Rituals and other religious practices, as well as meditation and metaphysical traditions are, undeniably, to a large extent similar, even identical. Concepts of sacred history and sources of religious authority are, however radically different and justify the claim of the Bonpo's to constitute an entirely distinct religious community" (Kvaerne 1995, 13).

Karmay

In *A Historical Overview of the Bon Religion* Samten Karmay, director of research in history and anthropology at the National Centre of Scientific Research in Paris notes as his finding:

> *"There was no such teaching in Tibet as 'pure' as some Tibetan Buddhist might like to claim. In other words Bon and Tibetan Buddhism are like two sides of the same coin – on viewing one must also turn it over to see what is on the other side"* (Karmay 2007, 55).

In the article Karmay points at another important issue. He stresses that so far much research focuses at developments that can be observed from monastic orders. And monastic traditions in particular are dominant in many research projects. But especially in the Bon the passing on and safeguarding of the religious praxis is the domain of families (laymen and teachers). In much research this tradition was and is overlooked, resulting in a misshapen image (Karmay 2007, 55-64).

This means that a part of the history and growth of the Bon as a religion has not yet been disclosed or explained, and that the position of women and nuns has been underexposed.

More attention given to the importance of family lines and lines of ancestry and the part played by women in the lines of ancestry might cast a different light on both place and position of women and on the religious positions they hold in the community.

1.2.4 Scholarly Research into Nuns and Women in the Bon

If the Bon and Tibetan Buddhism are considered to be two sides of the same coin, the story of nuns and women in the Bon threatens to become lopsided. Research related to the position of nuns and women is directly linked to Tibetan Buddhism. Specific research into the position of nuns and women in the Bon has not come to my knowledge.

The past ten to fifteen years biographies have been published of well-known women practising religion, providing images and insights of the lives of these extraordinary women. What remains, however, is the question whether they should be regarded as a paradigm for every day life of nuns and women. At least until 1959 Tibetan history mentions various kinds of religiously practising women: female oracles* and soothsayers, minstrels, women inside the tantric praxis (Yogini*) and nuns (Willis 1987, 98).

Narratives about or scholarly research into the role and position of women, both secular and religious, from the years before the rise of Buddhism, are rarely found in Tibet.

It is commonly known that in those days matriarchal communities did exist in the regions that now form Tibet, or used to fall under Tibetan dominance. There is mention of influential queens and of ancestral lines passed on through female lineage (Gyasto 1987, 34-35).

In the pantheon of both Buddhism and the Bon many goddesses are found, and several religious practices require the presence of both the male and the female element. Tibet is known for the development of a form of Buddhism that includes a female principle, probably also under Bon influence.

Rita Gross noticed that Buddhism in Tibet came across a community that offered its women more choice than women in neighbouring countries, even though religious power was in the hands of men (Gross 1993, 85).

Evidently women were allowed to exercise religious practices diverse levels, although they appear not to have held the same position as men. Once again I want to emphasise that these perspectives and findings are and were studied using Buddhist viewpoints.

In the 11th century the Bon starts to set up a series of monasteries and simultaneously a monastic tradition begins to take shape (Kvaerne 1995, 17).

The monastic tradition of the Bon is organised along the same lines as Buddhism. It is a matter of course that the monastic tradition for women, started in the same period, followed the same principles.

Nonetheless there are differences between the monastic traditions of the Bon and Buddhism, notably where the basic principles are concerned. The history of Indian Buddhism tells that the Buddha was not eager to allow women to take part in monastic life. It was Ananda who persuaded him, accepting the condition that women were never to fully enter the religious community, actually remaining a life long novice. On entering a monastery women are asked to take an extra number of vows, concerning their behaviour towards men, even though Buddhist scriptures make clear that in Karmic* terms there is no strict difference between men and women. It is assumed that these rules were meant to adapt Buddhist rules to the Indian society of those days.[1] The conditions apply to Buddhist nuns till the present day.

The Bon is different, in that respect. Its rules stipulate that nuns can receive a full ordination. This emerges from its earliest history. Legend says that Tonpa Sherab, the founder of the Bon, did not distinguish between men and women. When revealing his teachings, the men sat to his right and the women to his left. In this oral teaching he initiated both men and women. The initiation is passed on through family lines and the authority bestowed on this myth makes it possible to give women a full ordination as a nun.

What does this starting point mean for the position of nuns in present day Tibet?

In 1984 the Council for Religious and Cultural Affairs of the Dalai Lama carried out an investigation of the number of nunneries in Tibet before 1959. The study found a total of 618 convents. It is remarkable, however, that nunneries of the Bon were not included in the study (Tsomo 1987, 119).

---

1   Lecture notes *Spirituality of Buddhism*, 9 May 2007, by dr. Paul J.C.L. van der Velde, Radboud University Nijmegen.

Monastic life for men and women is organised along different lines. As a rule nunneries and monasteries are set up apart, though some Buddhist sects follow their own rules.

The following forms of organisation are found in Tibetan monastic life (Havenik, 1999, 42):

- <u>Large, nationally organised monasteries</u>, attracting monks from all over Tibet who take part in a training eventually leading to the Geshe degree. In Tibet these monasteries are not accessible for women.

- <u>Local or regional monasteries</u>. Both monasteries and convents are found in this category. Teaching is a primary activity in these institutions and often there is a strong connection with the local and/or regional population. Men and women come to the monasteries for advice and rituals and it is the task of many monks and nuns to teach them. In hierarchal respect the nunneries often are subordinate to the local monasteries. It is known, however, that as an exception to the rule a number of convents in Tibet used to be led by an abbess. Nuns do learn to read and write, and in some convents they follow philosophy classes. Within the walls of a monastery a hierarchical structure prevails and tasks and duties are handed out. Performing rituals is often the primary task of nuns.

- <u>Smaller monasteries (hermitages*)</u> are the cloisters where men and women find recluse to lead a life dedicated to meditation and religious praxis. As for Bon there is hardly any information available, though.

During my visit to Tibet (2006) and my fieldwork in India I received information that supports the idea that the Bon has convents in the last two categories. Conclusive information about the number of convents is not available, but accounts I collected during the fieldwork estimate their number between four and ten.

Women did play a role and held positions in religious life in Tibet, but that picture remains sketchy and underexposed where the Bon is concerned.

1.3 Objective of Research

This historical survey of the Bon and Tibet makes clear that many questions remain unanswered. Research into place and position of women in Tibetan society and their role inside the religious system was carried out mainly from Buddhist perspectives. Starting points and conclusions may very well disagree with the situation inside the Bon.

Unlike Buddhism the Bon claims that the position of the nuns and monks is similar. In spite of this clear vantage point, it turns out to be very difficult to find written accounts about the position of nuns in the Bon tradition. By carrying out research at a micro level among the nuns of Redna Menling, the first and so far only Bon convent in exile, I wanted to gain insight in their lives. Why do young women choose for a life as a nun? From what background do they come to that choice and which future do they envisage for themselves inside the Bon religious praxis?

I meant to use their narratives as a means to gain insight in the place and position of the nuns in the Bon community in general and more specific in the monasterial tradition of Dolanji/Redna Menling, but also in the world in which this religious community has its place (Bon community, Tibet, the world). I found a lively interaction between this religious community, the world in which this community manifests itself, and the individuals concerned. By mapping these interactions I set out to clarify its influence on place and position of each nun.

1.4 Research Questions

These considerations resulted in the following concrete research questions:

What is a nun's place in the Bon religion?
- Why do young women decide the become a nun
- What meaning do the women give to monasterial life
- What role did women play in the history of the Bon
- Which connections and influences may be observed at these different levels?

1.5 Methods and my Role as a Scholarly Researcher

The lack of research into the position of nuns inside the Bon reduced the scope of available sources to work founded on research among Tibetan Buddhist nuns. It is however the separate origin, claimed by the Bon and leading to a special attitude towards the position of nuns, that made me decide to not develop a theoretical concept before starting my fieldwork.

This approach resulted in qualitative fieldwork, where observations, annotations and the interviews I held, form the data to work with. This way a foundation is laid for the development of theoretical concepts. My aim was to procure acceptation as a member of the group I was going to observe. I have chosen for a moderate type of participant observation, because I did not have sufficient time to effectively master all activities of the group.

I was not a stranger to the Dolanji Bon community. I had visited the Menri Monastery the past years a number of times in several capacities. But always as a member of a group or accompanied by my partner, never as a researcher.

The relation between the lay community and religious persons is shaped mainly through reciprocity. In Tibet the community supports a monastery and the monasterial community takes care of the needs of the common people by providing prayers, rituals, education and advice. Absence of a large community of common people in exile is the reason that a part of these services are now provided for by Western organisations and individual persons who feel connected to the world of the Bon. In the wake of the organisation of my partner I have been a regular visitor of the Menri Monastery during recent years. My personal and scholarly interest for the Bon and the role of its nuns was well known.

The fact that my research was especially aimed at the community of nuns has had other consequences. Nuns have taken many vows and are held to observe certain rules of life. Lacking the intention to become a nun, I had to accept that becoming a member of the research group was going to be an illusion. I wished to take part in daily life in the convent, if as possible and allowed. Those were boundaries defining my position and role as an active observer.

Chapter 2

The Bon | A Community in Exile

2.1 Introduction

"We had nothing, not even a bar of soap to wash and clean our children, so I went out begging for a small peace of soap. But the people of Dolanji did not have anything themselves." [2]

When China occupied Tibet in 1959 many Tibetan men, women, children, including members of the religious communities fled to India. Refugee camps were set up at the foot of the Himalayas with the aid of the Indian government and international organisations. The central Tibetan administration numbered 46 Tibetan settlements in India, Nepal and Bhutan in 2000 and a total of 100.541 Tibetan refugees dispersed in Southern Asia (Bernstorff, 2003). Among them many Bonpos. A large group of Tibetans, however, found an abode in America and Europe. The largest community in the Western world, 1806 refugees, is found in Switzerland, where they were admitted between 1960 and 1996.

2.2 The Bon Community in Dolanji

After their flight from Tibet many Bonpo's are put to work, building roads as navvies in Kulu-Manali, India. It is hard work under harsh conditions. Many men and women die. By the mid-sixties the Bon in exile succeeds in reorganising itself and all efforts are aimed at realising a more permanent place of settlement. Land is acquired in Dolanji (close to Solan-Himalay Pradesh) in 1967 and in the same year the Tibetan Bonpo Foundation is registered. Some 70 families settle in Dolanji. They are allotted a piece of land to build themselves a house. The times are hard; the general shortage of funds prevents starting up a stream of building activities. In these early years there is a lack of everything, food in particular. Special shelters are set up for the children, where they receive education in their own language and culture.

Among the children spending their youth in a hostel in Dharamsala was Tashi Tsomo. *"Life in the hostel in Dharamsala was not easy. There was lack of everything, even food and water. Children died there because there was not enough food and water."* [3] Tashi now lives with her family in Dolanji, where she takes care of her mother.

---

2   Fieldnotes, conversation with Lama Khemsar Rinpoche*, 2 September 2007.
3   Fieldnotes, conversation with Tashi Tsomo, 21 September 2007.

Figure 2.1: Diagram of the Organisation

The settlement was named Thobgyel Sarpa, originally the name of a village close to the Menri Monastery in Tibet. During the period in Kulu-Manali the spiritual leader of the Bon, by tradition the abbot of the Menri Monastery, dies. The ceremony to decide on his succession had to wait until 1969. Then Sangye Tendzin Jongdong, a monk working at the University of Oslo, was chosen to be the new spiritual leader and become the 33rd abbot of Menri. On his installation he was given the names of Lungtok Tenpai Nyima.

The following years much effort is put into building activities, in the village, at the temple and housing for the monks. The name for the new monastic complex is Bonpo Monastic Center and it is situated around the Menri Monastery that derives its name from the monastery in Tibet that constituted the religious centre of the Bon.

The religious community, the only Bon community in exile, can roughly be divided into three groups. In the first group the monks and Lama's who fled from Tibet are found. They perform religious temple ceremonies for the inhabitants of the village, private ceremonies are held in the homes of the people. In general this group contributes to all activities and rituals, which are part of living and working in a monastery.

A second group consists of 35 young men who have taken their vows in the first years of the new monastery in exile. Training for Geshes has started, opening the possibility to follow a full religious program in exile.

Boys from seven to fourteen years make up the third group. They go to the secular primary school in the village, but also take part in temple ceremonies. The monks of the monastery have a special teaching program for these boys who have a home in the Bon Children Welfare Center. Though some came out of their own will, most boys were sent to Dolanji by their parents and will in due course take the vows leading to a religious life.

The monastic system follows Tibetan rules. The monastery is not just a religious centre; it is also a place for traditional education and culture. When set up, it lacked special facilities for nuns. As time passes both the secular and the religious services are increased. This results in homes for boys and for girls, meant to shelter the many orphans in de community. But it also is a place for children smuggled across the Tibetan border into India. In this way the children do not only receive education, but also have also free access to the Bon culture and tradition ((Skorupski 1981).

Like other Tibetan communities the Bon community has found its place in Hindu dominated Indian society. Where Tibetan exiles are concerned India has applied two important principles: in the first place a liberal and open attitude, not aimed at complete assimilation of the Tibetans in the Indian society, and secondly acknowledgement of the leadership of the Dalai Lama in both religious and political respect. These principles enabled the Tibetans to maintain the quintessence of their cultural, religious and political autonomy (Norbu 2003, 204).

The first years in exile the Bon community had to rely most of all on mutual assistance, as there was no Tibetan government in exile that could lend support (Kind 1995). This attitude underlines that indeed it is a matter of two separate religions, which in Tibet were not always on a friendly footing. But this also reveals two separate identities. Mariette Kind gives the following description:

"The struggle for the official recognition of the Bonpo shows the dynamics in the exiled Tibetan community. In spite of repeated requests it took seventeen years until a representative of the Bonpo was allowed to join the 'Assembly of Tibetan peoples

Deputies'. The main reason for this long delay was the reluctance of the Tibetan administration to recognise a religious movement that considered itself pre-Buddhist and might weaken the authority of the Buddhist leadership" (Kind 1995, 9).

For the exiled Bon however recognition was important in order to acquire access to a humane life for both laymen and those practising religion, while in exile.

"Nowadays tolerance towards the Bonpo is growing. Especially the second generation of Tibetans, politically striving for a democratic ideal, shows more and more acceptance. Observation of the first and second generations of exiles reveals a transformation process that supports a dynamic view of the notion of identity. The positive image brought about by official recognition has led to a strengthening of the self-confidence of the Bonpo. Building activities of new monasteries in Nepal and Sikkim show that the tradition has received a new impulse. Recently even a first Bon center was founded in the West, in Houston in de USA. The revitalising is also visible in several border areas of Nepal, such as Dolpo, where Geshes graduated in Dolanji rekindle the religion" (Kind 1995, 10).

The ties with the Western world have tightened, the past twenty years. The growing interest for Buddhism, and in its wake for the Bon, have given an impetus in several countries to set up foundations which foster the advancement of the Bon teachings, but at the same time aims to raise funds for the support of the monasteries and their inhabitants.

The Menri Monastery is the official seat of the Bon in exile. In the beginning the monks were exiles from Tibet, but as the years of exile lengthened monks from Nepal, Bhutan and India joined them in Dolanji. In recent years even men from France, Poland and Mongolia have come to Dolanji to take their vows as a monk, and sometimes also to follow the Geshe training.

Geshes from the first group in exile were invited to the West, initially the USA, to bring interested parties in contact with the Bon and its spiritual and religious techniques, such as meditation. Most of the contacts in America were established with the support of the Healing Light Center of reverend Rosalyn L. Bruyere. Bruyere works as a healer and a psychic channel. She claims to have contact, as a channel, with a spirit who declares to be a Bon monk. The group in front of whom she channelled this monk, started to search for the origins of this religion that was new to all of them. Halfway the eighties they found the Bon community in Dolanji. They set up an exchange, which culminated in a comprehensive ceremony for the inauguration of Rosalyn Bruyere as an oracle of the Bon in America in December 1998. This ceremony relates to a legend that that still is told in Dolanji. The 21st abbot of the Menri Monastery is said to have foretold that the Bon was to be saved by a 'white women from the West'. When Rosalyn Bruyere and the Bon made contact, the prophecy was realized. The Bon had 'arrived' in the West. [4]

---

4   See Appendix 2: letter Vasilka Nicolva and John Barnett.

The past few years Dolanji saw the assembly of a guesthouse, a school, a library and new quarters for the monks. Also the children's home was refurbished. These projects were all funded with donations from the West. Healthcare for the inhabitants of Dolanji is in the hands of teams of physicians and dentists from Canada and the USA, who visit the village a few times every year. But traditional Tibetan medicine is also encouraged. One day every month a Tibetan doctor has surgery in the village.

In 2007 346 Tibetan Bonpo lived in the village and some 500 children attended the school. The children are housed in the Bon Children Home, the Redna Menling Convent or the Bon Children Welfare Center, which belongs to the community of monks in the village. The administrative office of the Tibetan Bonpo Foundation in Dolanji estimates 150 monks and 19 nuns have a permanent abode in the monasteries.

Both the secular and the religious community have found a place in the predominant Hindu region. Apart from some minor incidents the Bon and the Hindu inhabitants get along peacefully. I myself came to the following conclusion:

> *"Actually I most enjoy the early mornings when I get up at about half past five. I brew my coffee and settle at about six on the balcony with a warm scarf and a cardigan to watch the nuns light the sang fires. Soon the sacrificial smoke rises from the sites next to the houses in the village. At six o'clock a thin loudspeaker resounds the tones of Hindu music, usually proclaiming a Hindu festivity. By six thirty the bell rings to announce the daily ritual of the blessing of the water at the house of His Holiness. Half an hour later in the hostel the children start to recite their prayers or mantras. At that time the first Indian inhabitants leave their homes. But only at half past eight the streets start to fill with people."*[5]

In his article *'The Settlements: Participation and Integration in the Tibetan Diaspora'* Dawa Norbu reaches the conclusion that the Tibetans have succeeded in adapting very well to their Indian environment. The use of Indian labour in building and agriculture activities by both the monasteries and non-religious persons has started an economic exchange (Norbu 2003, 204-205). This also was the case in Dolanji, where building activities were flourishing the past years. At first the monks did the building themselves, but more recently Indians were contracted to do the job.

Dolanji is divided into four areas. Most eye-catching is the entry gate, showing the name of the village in Tibetan script. On either side are small shops, a restaurant and public telephone booths. The Menri Monastery, the temples and the quarters of the monks form the centre of Dolanji, the family houses are assembled in the village, a bit more downhill. A strip of land separates the village and the monastery. On the strip the secular activities find place. There the administration building is located, the health clinic, and several smaller workshops, such as the carpentry shop, the farm and the guesthouse. The school was built between the village and the river. It is a hilly terrain, more or less cut in two by a river. Across the river, physically separated from the rest of the village, the nunnery was erected.

---

5   Fieldnotes, 17 September 2007.

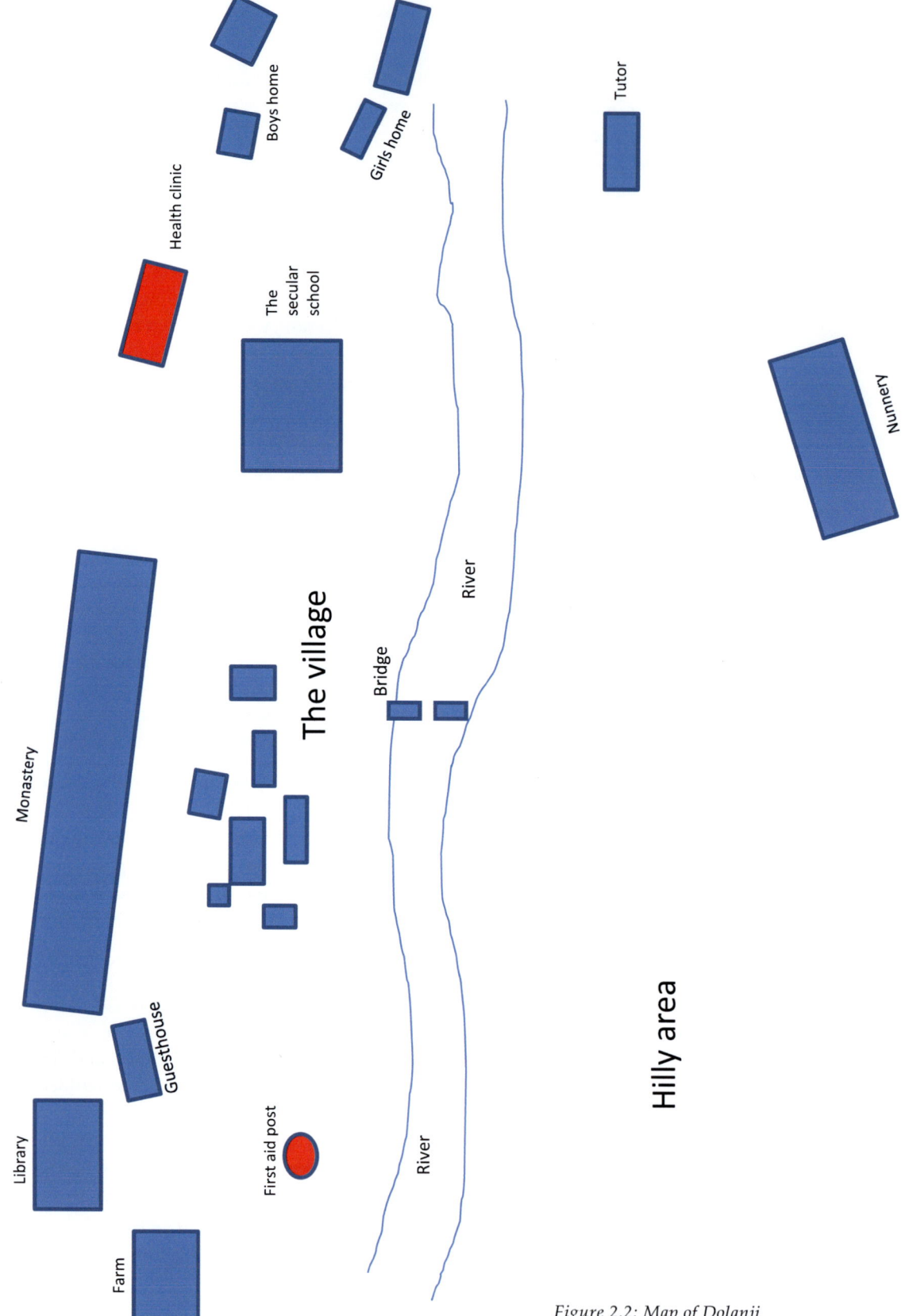

Figure 2.2: Map of Dolanji

Figure 2.3: View of the Menri Monastery from Redna Menling

Figure 2.4: View of Redna Menling from the Menri Monastery

Several Indian villages surround Dolanji. Dolanji itself has a number of small shops catering for the first primary needs. For everything else the people have to go Solan, much larger with 22.000 inhabitants. There is a bus service running twice a day.

His Holiness Lungtok Tenpai Nyima is the leader of both religious and secular life in Dolanji. The religious community has come a long way, from Zhang Zhung, the cradle of the Bon, to Tibet and India and at last making contact with the West. This last development in particular, awakens mixed views and feeling in the community. It is striking however that in geographical and historical respects Zhang Zhung sometimes is thought to have been in what now is called Himachal Pradesh, where Dolanji is found.

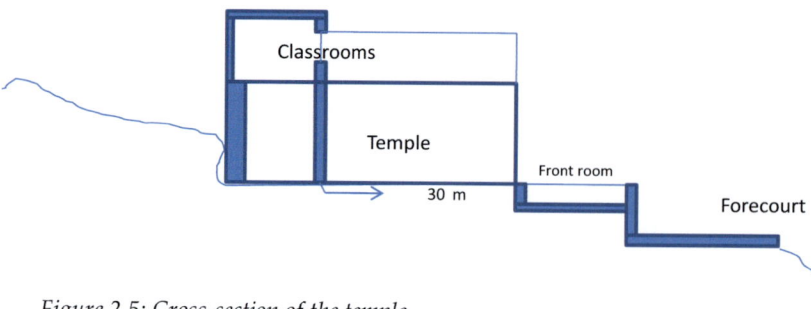

Figure 2.5: Cross-section of the temple

On the one hand the Bon community regards this increase in contacts, enabling growth of the community, with respect and gratefulness. On the other hand these foreign influences are looked upon with reserve and care. In an interview His Holiness phrased these mixed feelings in this way:

> *"Desire arises, very much desire. If the monks and Geshes receive good education and good training, and they stay in the monastery, follow their classes and do the praxis, they are safe. But we leave for Western countries to take up teaching there. Then more desire arises, and more wishes. Sometimes they marry and follow that path. Then everything is reduced. It is not only a sacred path, the path may also lead the wrong way."*[6]

Since the first days in exile the community has made every effort to protect its authenticity and identity, while adapting to a changing environment and changing influences. The authenticity and identity is laid down in concepts such as keeping the teaching pure. Stories about other convents, where nuns are said to wear or receive jewellery, are being told with evident disapproval. Much attention is also placed on the fact that what counts in the end is not the number of nuns or monks living in the monastery. What does count is that the monks and nuns present are focussed on the religious praxis and take that task seriously.

Just as it is impossible to consider the Bon without taking into account the history and development of Buddhism in Tibet, is impossible to consider the Bon without taking into account and interpret the influence of the developments in exile. The history shows that the Bon is capable of adapting to changing circumstances. Even though, as the words of His Holiness illustrate, this is often a difficult assignment for the religious community.

2.2.1 The Community of Nuns in Dolanji

Building the Redna Menling convent, 'the land of the precious medicine' was started in 2003. Western sponsors donated most of the funds. Special attention was given to the design of the buildings, so that they remind as much as possible of the Tibetan tradition. It had to be clear that this is a Tibetan Bon-monastery, quite distinct from the Hindu temples in the vicinity.

---

6   Interview with His Holiness Lungtok Tenpai Nyima, 1 September 2007.

The temple is the centre of the complex; with on either side the dormitories of the nuns. The kitchen and the community room are located on the left side of the temple (see illustration on page 22). From the main entrance of the temple one has a beautiful view of the valley, including the Menri temple complex across the river.

Before the convent was consecrated, the religious community of Dolanji did not include nuns. There were some nuns indeed, but these women made their vows at a ripe age after retiring from traditional family life. They live on their own, or in the shelter of their family, as is quite common in Tibet. Women may take their vows and practise a religious life while remaining in their family. Data from the Tibetan government in exile disclose a total of 1290 Buddhist nuns in exile in India and Nepal: 916 live in a convent and 374 stay with their families (Tsomo 2003, 346).

We may distinguish of two distinct streams of refugees to India and Nepal. The first started immediately after the events of 1959, the second reached its summit between 1989 and 1993. Although there never was a significant stream of nuns fleeing from Tibet, a recent increase in the number of nuns in exile is evident. Most of them are born in exile and it is the prospect of good education and training that appears to be a strong stimulus (Tsomo 2003, 346-347).

At first there were no nuns in the Dolanji community, but there are unofficial stories of women travelling all the way from Tibet to come and take their vows in Dolanji, returning to Tibet afterwards or embarking on a pilgrimage. Hannah Havnevik tells such a story in 'Tibetan Buddhist nuns' (Havnevik 1999, 100). While in Dolanji I wanted to know more about this nun, but there was not really anyone who knew where she went or what she had done after taking her vows. One of my contacts suspects that she may have died.

One of the Geshes I have interviewed, told that his sister had taken her vows and hopes to find a religious career. She doesn't live in the convent in Dolanji. She stays either in America, or she moves in with her mother in Kathmandu. After graduating from university this young woman found out that the Dolanji nunnery couldn't offer her a fitting prospective. She hopes that living in America will give her full command of English, so that in due time she may set up a Bon center for women in America or Europe.

In some of the interviews I had, I heard about a Bon-monastery in Kathmandu. It is a monastery for men, but there are some ten nuns living in the direct vicinity.

living outside the nunnery	
Tibet	2
living in the nunnery	
India, Kinnoor	2
Nepal, Dolpo	44
Tibet	1

Table 2.6: Place of origin of the nuns and girls in Dolanji

The religious life of a Bon nun may start at an early age. Often a family decides to put a very young girl in care of a convent. At about 14 such a girl has to decide whether she really wants to become a nun and pursue a religious career.

At the time of my fieldwork 47 women and girls were living in Redna Menling convent, while the total number of persons registered was 49.

> *"No, I've never been to school. We have many sheep at home and there is a lot of work to do when they have to be shaved. Taking care of the wool is a girl's job. Trying to do business is for the boys. My father works in the fields and it is our task to water the crops, while my mother looks after the herds, the cattle. The cattle need milking, and after that it is time for making cheese. It is a remote village, actually we are nomads. Our work follows the two seasons. I can't read or write, but at home we speak Tibetan."*[7]

This quote is a fair illustration of the way almost all nuns portrays the place where they were born and grew up.

Historically Dolpo belongs to the sphere of influence of Western Tibet, that is the region where the kingdom of Zhang Zhung is thought to have been and where the Bon partly originated. *One of the first scholarly descriptions of Dolpo is from the hand of David Snellgrove in* 'Himalayan Pilgrimage'. *Snellgrove sketches a remote region, bereft of most modern amenities. During his pilgrimage he visits both Buddhist and Bon monasteries and concludes that the Bon is still strong and vivid in Dolpo.*

Comparing Buddhist and Bon literature and ceremonies, Snellgrove finds out that assimilation has taken place in both religions (Snellgrove 1961). In her article Mariette Kind comes to the conclusion that Dolpo in particular is flourishing, and especially where the monastic tradition is concerned (Kind 1995).

The community of nuns, as it has evolved since 1993 is a very young community. Both in arranging things and in religious affairs the community relies on the support of the Menri Monastery. The monastery and the community in Redna Menling runs a very clear line of separation in the form of the river. This has been a deliberate choice. When the plans for a convent started to take shape, several lots in Dolanji were taken into consideration. Among the vows nuns and monks take are vows to live in celibacy. The physical separation evidently is meant to anticipate problems in that area, for both men and women.

2.3 The Set-up of the Project

My fieldwork is by nature qualitative interpretative (see 1.5.1). The basic principle of this method is the description and the value attributed by people in daily life to their environment. This places great significance on the access of the researcher to the experiences of the participants and their description of life as it hits to them. In my case the participants were the nuns and other members of the Dolanji religious community.

---

[7] Interview, Ani Monlam Wangmo, 6 September 2007.

The presentation and analysis of my findings form the foundation of the theoretical concept that offers an answer to my research question (see 1.4). The most important tools of research I used were participating observations and interviews.

2.3.1 Observations

When setting up my fieldwork I had intensive contact with His Holiness, in order to prepare my coming to Dolanji as good as possible. It was about key matters such as access to sources of information, housing and support in the person of an interpreter/translator.

When drafting the fieldwork I expected to stay a month in the guesthouse and a month in the nunnery. As I could not predict where the last information was to be collected, I decided not to choose yet between the nunnery and the guesthouse.

The guesthouse is a neutral site, allowing reasonable freedom of action. Life in the convent is strictly ruled by regulations and etiquette. In order to be able to collect as much information as possible and to approach the subject from different angles, I assumed taking an abode in both the guesthouse and the convent would be the best solution. In the end I decided to skip the convent, after it turned out the living there involved too many health risks at that moment. I decided on a moderate form of participating observation, because a period of three months turned out to be not long enough to immerse completely in daily life and fully master every custom.

The introductory period I spend alternating in the Menri Monastery, the guesthouse and the nunnery. The next month and a half I daily made the trip to the nunnery, to spend the whole day there and sometimes a part of the evening. In that way I succeeded in taking part in the daily routine of life in the nunnery. My aim was to balance the perspectives from the inside and the outside, thus achieving a sound and guaranteed way of gathering information.

Observation Sites

Both the religious and the lay community of Dolanji are rather small, so that the presence of a Westerner is quite conspicuous. Guests, however, are regularly seen in the village. They may seek spiritual development; they may have come on behalf of supportive projects, or visiting their next of kin in the monastery or the village. And there is a regular influx of visitors from all over the world. All of them find shelter in the guesthouse, run by Geshe Sonam who tries to find an answer to all needs and wishes of these temporary inhabitants.

On arrival the abbot takes care of me at first, but Geshe Sonam gradually takes over from him.

An advantage of being introduced as a guest by the abbot is that one finds many open doors in the community. On the other hand the abbot's authority is so great that no one is likely to ignore his wishes.

As a rule the temple is off limits to laymen, and inhabitants of the village will not enter there. But Westerners do and on normal days this is more or less condoned. However, when special ceremonies are to be performed, even curious guests are not allowed to enter the temple.

The abbot regularly stimulated me to visit the temple. I preferred to do the Kor'-Ra*, the walk around the temple, early in the morning in the company of some women from the village.

The main temple and its direct surroundings are the domain of the monks. A Western woman attracts a lot of attention and her merely being there might embarrass people. The temple courts are linked up with the quarters of the monks and the places where they have their classes. That is why I had the feeling that it was not a place where I should linger.

I thought it best to meet the persons who were to inform me about life in Dolanji and its cloisters in the office of the Bon. That seemed a fairly neutral alternative. The route from the guesthouse to the convent passes through the village, past the school and the medical station. After some time the inhabitants of the village grew accustomed to me and addressed me as *Ani-La. Ani** is the title to address a nun and *La* is used for greeting a respected person. Once I passed the first training people said *Ani-La, Ani Gompa?,* meaning 'are you going to the convent, sister?' Few people in the village do speak English, so spontaneous contacts were rare. After some time I met with Tashi Tsomo. She helped me translating the interviews and became an important source of information. Also the fact that her family more or less took me in, made walking about in the village more easy. The small shops, the juice bar and the restaurant at the entrance of the village were places where I could hang out discreetly to watch Tibetan and Indian village life intermingle.

Talking with hands and feet I managed to get by in the nunnery. One of the nuns did speak English quite well and I am glad I could depend on her when it came to understand all sorts of events. The nuns are used to receive visitors and guide them through the convent, serving tea and, if possible, answering questions. In the beginning my arrival and taking part in the daily routines gave rise to some confusion, because it ignored the way they felt one should accommodate a guest. This feeling was accentuated by the extreme circumstances that dominated my first period in the convent. Extremely heavy rains washed away a part of the road to the convent. The first four weeks of my stay the nuns mustered an impressive effort in unblocking the road and restoring access to the convent. For me, being a participating observer, this meant joining the work force. I helped carrying stones, removing trees lying across the road, repairing holes. An unexpected situation that turned out to be a very good way of earning a place in the team.

The usual daily rhythm is centred around menial chores like cooking, cleaning, taking care of the toddlers, carrying out religious duties in the temple like prayers and rituals and daily classes about subjects taken from the Kanjur and Tanjur*.

For many nuns learning Tibetan also is a daily returning practice. Apart from that much time is devoted to self-study.

Collecting data

A small and handy notebook, always ready for scribbling down some notes was one of the things I always carried with me. Other things were a pencil and a pad to make sketches of situations. I worked out the fieldwork notes to the memo's that make up the backbone of this thesis.

In addition to the daily notes of the fieldwork I kept a diary, which included personal observations and feelings. Also, I filled in a logbook, keeping record of what I did during the daily and what I intended to do the next day. With these notes I tried to support my memory.

2.3.2 Interviews with Nuns and with Informants

Different kinds of interviews may be used in a research project, from interviews with leading questions to interviews with wide open questions. I decided to use a guide (Heldens & Reysoo 2005). Using a guide requires solid and meticulous preparation. The questions are made up in advance, even before starting the fieldwork. Preparation doesn't only include the subjects of questions, but may also elaborate on various aspects per subject. The guide is not just a list of subjects or questions about a subject; it also may include the introductions to questions and specify the subjects. Even while interviewing the answers are analysed, so that the interviewer may determine whether a subject is duly treated.

Another important reason to choose for working with a guide is that I had to rely on an interpreter or translator, as I speak neither Hindu nor Tibetan. Then a guide ensures a fine structure, which offers the possibility to uphold the focus of the interview in cooperation with the interpreter. English was spoken in the interviews with the prominent members of the community.

Collecting data

Before leaving for Dolanji I set up and worked out the interview guides for both the nuns and the key persons. Once in Dolanji I went through the interview guide for the nuns with Tashi Tsomo, in order to check whether they fitted in with their world of and vocabulary.

Thashi's comments and remarks prompted me to review certain questions, in particular the introductions of certain subject turned out to be too complex. Once we agreed I translated the interview into English. The interview guide for the nuns has four clusters:
1. Personal background and social setting in the country of origin.
2. Interaction between the biography and entering the convent.
3. Interaction between daily life in the convent and future prospects.
4. Ritual praxis and integration in daily life.

The four clusters of the interview guide for key persons are:
1. Personal background
2. History of the nun inside the Bon
3. Present situation of the nun inside the Bon

4. Future prospects of convents inside the Bon and Redna Menling in particular

Afterwards I made transcriptions of the digitally recorded interviews. During my stay in Dolanji I interviewed 18 nuns and 8 prominent members.

2.4 The group in Research

While preparing the fieldwork, it became evident that the group I was about to research was not going to be restricted to the nuns of Redna Menling. To gain insight in the position of nuns inside the community I also had to interview some prominent members. These were all Geshes, holding various positions and functions inside the Menri Monastery.

At the time of my fieldwork the nunnery numbered 47 inhabitants, 19 of who were reckoned to be within the limits of my research question. The group between 4 and approximately 16 years, though living in the nunnery, go to school and have not taken vows. After finishing school these children in principle have the choice to opt for a secular life.

Most of the children were given into the care of the convent by their parents or relatives. Three elder nuns, aged between 60 and 80, initially had a secular life, and only did choose for life in the convent at a ripe age. Two of these women do no live inside the convent. One lives on her own, the other lives with her son, a monk himself, next to the convent. The third nun, though living inside the convent, does not take part in its daily routines, such as menial chores and classes.

What remains is a group of 19 nuns, aged between 15 and 40, living permanently in the convent and familiar with the theme of my research.

2.4.1 Composition, Backgrounds and Daily Life

> "After sorting out the details of the nuns, I am amazed to find out that almost all of them come from Nepal. Not one of the nuns has a Tibetan background. I feel confused. What did I know about the Bon in Nepal, after all? Not much, to be honest."[8]

Of the 19 nuns in this group 17 are from the Nepalese Dolpo province. The other two were born in Kinnoor, India. And then there is one nun who turns out not to be in the convent at all. The management reports that she went back to Nepal to look after her sick father. The other nuns, however, tell me that she returned home and is not likely to come back.

No education	Went to school until 8 years	Went to school until 12 years	Graduated from secondary school
9	1	7	1

Table 2.7: Education

---

8   Fieldnotes, 15 August 2007.

40 years and more	From 23 to 40 years	From 16 to 22 years	15 years
1	2	14	1

Table 2.8: Age groups[9]

Bon family	Mixed Bon/Buddhist (mother Bon, father Buddhist)	Nyiamapa (oldest Buddhist sect, very similar to the Bon)	Buddhist (not belonging to a specific denomination)
9	1	6	3

Table 2.9: Religious background

The youngest nun entered the convent at 14, the oldest when she was 33 years old. Apart from the one who graduated from secondary school all nuns say that they had been helping out at home, working on the fields (agriculture and dairy farming) or helping in running the household. All had were assigned tasks in the house, took care of younger sisters and brothers or of a parent who stayed behind after divorce or the death of a partner. None of the women indicated having had a relation before entering the convent.

The mother tongue of the majority of the nuns is Tibetan or the Tibetan dialect spoken in one of the regions of Dolpo. All Nepalese nuns state that they are more or less fluent in Hindi.

In Dolanji nuns are addressed and address each other as Ani. The word Ani refers to an aunt in the family of the father. In Tibet, where I visited a nunnery in 2006, the title of a nun is jomo, referring to the female head of a family, or a mistress of the house, employing a servant. The official Tibetan title for a fully ordained nun is Gelongma; a woman ordained to be a novice is addressed as Getsulma. Tibetan Buddhism also uses the title Bhiksuni, which refers to a Buddhist nun who is ordained in Tibetan Buddhism.

The women I have interviewed have all taken the Geneyen* vows, the eight basic vows. Two of them had also taken the 25 Tsang Tsug* vows. All in all there are four different kind of vows: the Nye ne vows - the primary vows also taken by laymen, the Geneyen vows – taken by a monk or nun when ordained, the Tsang Tsug vows - an extension of the basic vows – and a special place is given to the Drang Song, the 243 vows monks take, and to the 360 vows of the Gelong, which are taken by nuns. All vows are laid down in the Vinaya*, the system of rules monks and nuns live by. In Redna Menling none of the nuns had (yet) taken all the vows.

Prior to taking the vows the head of a nun or monk is shaven. As long as a woman stays in the convent she will wear her hair short, as do the children who are given in the care of the convent. On entering the convent the women receive their robe, consisting of an underskirt and shirt, and an over shirt and skirt. A wrap also belongs to the nun's standard attire. When attending school, the chil-

---

9   Sometimes the age indicated leads to confusion, on the one hand because the Tibetan system of counting, starting with the moment of conception instead of the moment of birth, on the other hand because the registered age did not always was the factual age. Some nuns said they were older than the official registration. I have used the age given by the nuns themselves.

dren wear a uniform. Outside school, taking part in services in the temple or when carrying out rituals, they are dressed monastically.

The monastic dress code has different rules for winter and summer. The winter season formally starts on 1 December, but because of the exposure of the convent the winter robe usually appears in the autumn. The autumn in Dolanji is often cold and wet.

The Vinaya decrees that monks and nuns should keep their garments clean and tidy and are responsible for new clothes themselves. They usually earn the money needed by saying prayers and carrying out rituals. As a rule a family will support its religious members, if they have sufficient means. This is the case with some of the Nepalese nuns. The Tibetan government supplies a sum of money for monks and nuns that have fled from Tibet. On religious holy days all monks and nuns receive 50 rupees from the Menri Monastery.

These rules also apply to the Menri Monastery and only in special cases the monastery will lend support. In case of the nuns of Redna Menling, however, the Menri Monastery supplies all their needs, clothes included. This is a special arrangement.

Another possibility is that a nun is adopted by a sponsor. It means that the sponsor donates a monthly sum to the Menri Monastery. As a rule these donations are not used for the benefit of one person, but to cover general expenses. It is up to the sponsor to create a personal relationship with the nun in question, through letters or by coming to meet her. Building projects and large payments usually financed or paid for by funds collected abroad by one of the numerous Bon Foundations. During my fieldwork building activities for the nuns comprised new sleeping quarters, a thangka* workshop and a sewing shop.

Until now most nuns sleep in a large dormitory, together with the schoolchildren. Some nuns have smaller rooms, which they share with two or three children. There are few, if any, places where they can retire, because the terrain surrounding the convent is relatively small.

In the period of my fieldwork the nuns were mainly occupied learning the praxis of Chamma*, 'the loving mother', one of the most important goddesses in the Bon. She is the mother of all enlightened beings in the three times: past, present and future. Chamma is also called Yum Chen Sherab Chamma, and she is known to have a total of 21 different manifestations. Together these are called Chamma Nyer Chig (Dakpa 2003, 121). The praxis of Chamma comprises learning to recite the texts and prayers belonging to the 21 manifestations of Chamma. An important element of the praxis is learning to recite the so-called 'heart mantra's'.

When growing up none of the nuns in my research group had regular contact with the monastic tradition. That is why their training is not only about the religious subjects, but also explains the tasks found in a monastic tradition. The tasks to be fulfilled are:

- Gekö – keeper of discipline
  She keeps the control and the in the temple, and has the power to fine nuns who violate the rules

- Umtse – leader of prayers
  She leads the services in the temple and is the precentor in the prayers. When called for she plays the temple drum, which is found near the entrance of the temple.

- Chöpön – keeper of the altar
  She bears the responsibility for the daily offerings on the altar and looks after the altar in general.

- Treasurer
  She is responsible for the money the convent receives for the services rendered, like saying prayers.

- Ko Nyar – keeper of the keys
  She is in charge of the key to the temple and sounds the bell at every event: prayer, temple service, meals, and so on. She is also responsible for keeping the temple clean.

Figure 2.10: Ko Nyar - keeper of the keys

Figure 2.11: Domestic duties

Figure 2.12: Umtse – leader of prayers

Less official, but not less important are duties like operating the first aid post and watching over the medical supplies. These tasks rotate and are taken on for a year. The nun accountable for a certain task is always assisted by a second person. Which task a nun gets is decided by ballot. All nuns and girls over 14 years will vote, in a procedure supervised by the Lama and a committee of three wise women from the village. The Lama looks after the program of the daily classes of the nuns, but His Holiness is responsible for their religious training. The committee of the three wise women also oversees daily affairs in the convent, more or less as a kind of supervising body. During the time I stayed in the convent I did not learn to know them, because of illness or because they stayed outside Dolanji.

Nuns who do not have a special task, take turns when it comes to daily routines, such as preparing the meals of making tea. The food is supplied by Menri Monastery; as a rule the meals are sober and vegetarian. Fresh milk is every day available on the farm, next to the monastery. The farm, run by two Indian families, also supplies vegetables.

Three nuns are trained at the monastery to become Thangka painters. Thangka's are painted representations of saints from the Bon pantheon. In the months I lived in Dolanji much effort was put in the construction of a building that eventually is to become the workshop for Thangka painting.

One of the elder nuns looks after the small children and welcomes the guests. Three nuns have had first aid training and are qualified to treat minor injuries and health problems.

This is a general picture of a religious community in exile. In the beginning the community did not accommodate nuns. Only a few years ago profiling a monastic tradition for women started to receive attention for the first time. Why do women profess, how do they experience daily life in a nunnery? What colours these relations and how and in what way do they influence each other? These subjects I will treat extensively in the chapters to come.

Chapter 3

Reasons to profess | What makes a young woman become a nun?

3.1 Introduction

The continuing line in the interviews with the nuns is made up of three subjects:
- personal life story
- motives to enter the convent
- expectations

Chapter 3 focuses on what makes a young woman decide to profess, and what she expects from a life as a nun. Chapter 4 highlights life in a community of nuns, and the interactions between the nunnery and the Menri Monastery and with the lay community. But the attention also touches on the future expectations of the nuns and how these expectations reflect the exiled Bon community and the relations of the nuns with the world around them.

While preparing for my fieldwork my views were strongly influenced by what I knew and had read so far about women in and from Tibet. All stories about women elevated way above and beyond daily life: holy women. They are unique because of the life they have led or because of their extraordinary merits, their special gifts. Or when it comes to the Bon tradition, a lineage that is regarded to be holy. Their biographies mirror an idealised life. Accounts of the life of an average nun are rare and for all I know there are no (auto-) biographies of Bon nuns.

Metaphors created this way do not necessarily reflect reality. This is what Ido Abram identifies as an image: a forced identity (Abram 2006, 13). By inviting the nuns to tell their personal stories I hope to clarify the influences and circumstances that contributed to their decision to become a nun, its meaning in terms of their daily life and the effect on the Bon community where until recently nuns were hardly visible.

Telling stories is a typical human habit. That is why man is also called homo narrans – the story telling man. When we feel the need to express ourselves, telling a story is one of the means we resort to. Such a story opens the path leading to our inner world and reveals how we see and experience the world around us.

A story reveals our identity, as it is displayed to the outside world. Telling our personal story to someone else sets an exchange in motion, in which we may discover ourselves. We gain insight in life and in what we call personal identity. Identity is not a static phenomenon; it develops in interaction, while talking to others. Each story has its own context. When I sit and talk to a friend, I am unlikely to tell my story in the same way as when I were to use it in a counselling session. In that way we present different aspects of our self, of our own identity. It is how we tell about the experiences of our personal identity, about a life taking shape and about the cultural context in which it finds its shape and becomes manifest (Lieblich 1998, 7-9).

The meaning of stories and of telling stories surpasses the individual. Its function, sometimes only evident while the story is told, may be social, political and sometimes even economical. Stories have a deep influence on the way people form concepts in relation to a chosen subject: in my case Tibetan nuns. Such an exchange between the individual and the world around him or her may trigger changes taking place inside a community. In other words, a story that is told could move its audience, initiating eventual changes in that community.

Bearing that in mind, I started my series of interviews and I listened to the stories of the nuns of Redna Menling.

Three issues formed the backbone of the interview-guide: *life stories, motives and expectations.* Piloted by these issues I went to work with the four clusters of questions:
1. Personal background and social circumstances in the country of origin (3.2)
2. The relation between the life story and entering the convent (3.3)
3. The relation between daily life and the expectations of life as a nun (3.4)
4. Religious praxis and integration in daily life (4.1)

Together the first three clusters make up the quintessence of this chapter. The fourth is treated in chapter 4.

3.2 Personal and Social Background in the Country of Origin

Every woman walks her own unique path when it comes to entering a convent. Yet common elements are found in the stories of the nuns. In general it is unusual for an oldest child to become a monk or nun, as it may hinder prolongation of the lineage of the family and the passing down of family property. The oldest son is the first in line and in absence of a male heir property may be passed down to the oldest daughter.

Oldest child	Youngest child	Only child	Others
5	2	1	10

Table 3.1: Position in the family

Both parents died	Both parents still alive	Mother died	Father died	Parents divorced
1	10	4	2	1

Table 3.2: Parents of the nuns

Nuns who are an oldest daughter, though not the oldest child often have to wait to profess until the marriage of the oldest son has brought a daughter-in-law into the family. Samten tells how it worked for her:

> *"I am the oldest of the girls. All my sisters are younger than me. Being the oldest daughter I always had to help my mother with her work in the fields and with looking after the cattle. Because of this I didn't go to school. But now my brother has married and his wife lives in our house. She now helps my parents. And I was able to come here."* [10]

All nuns make clear that they grew up in their own family, a nuclear family with a father and a mother, brothers and sisters. Tsundu lost both her parents. She was 3 when her mother died. On the death of her father, when she was 13, she joined the family of her oldest brother.

Most nuns come from remote regions in Nepal, from small villages with an average of ten to twenty families. Other family members, such as grandparents, uncles and aunts often live close by, not more than a day's walking. Most families earn their livelihood as farmers and as a rule the nuns had to help out working in the fields or herding the cattle.

In general the mother is responsible for the work in the field, the father for the cattle – yaks and horses, often kept for trading. Even the two nuns whose fathers were employed, had to work in the fields. Lobsang, born and raised in India, finished secondary school. She is the only nun who did not have to work at home. Her father served in the Tibetan army and her mother worked as a civil servant in the Indian administration.

Rinchen Sangmo tells about daily life at home and the work that needed to be done there:

> *"There was no school where we lived, so I never went to school. I worked at home. Herding the cattle, working in the fields, and fetching water, that was exhausting. And I had to weave and make clothes. I worked with the loom. We are farmers. Because the farm is very remote, trade is very difficult. But we could cater for ourselves. We grew everything we needed."* [11]

Most nuns see the economic environment in which they grew up as neither poor nor rich (*"our needs were met"*). Two nuns tell about the estates and the large stocks of cattle owned by their families, and in doing so they distinguish themselves as from an economical rich background. Only one nun classifies the economic situation of her family as poor. She indicates that the early death of her father resulted in the loss of a steady income.

Nuns from Bon-families often can rely on a network of relatives in Dolanji, such as professed brothers in the monastery, or brothers, sisters or cousins staying in one of the hostels and going to school in Dolanji. Monks who actually are not akin, but come from the same region, are often regarded as relatives.

---

10   Interview, Ani Samten Wangmo, 27 September 2007.
11   Interview, Ani Rinchen Sangmo, 5 September 2007.

In this way the frequent family ties with the Lopan* are based on belonging to the same lineage. In general the nuns feel they are raised in a religious setting, though that feeling is strongest in Bon-families. The monasteries in the vicinity of the native villages of the nuns usually are monasteries for men. The ties with these monasteries range from very close to a vague notion that somewhere over there, there is a monastery.

The nuns tell much about rituals, carried out at home or in the village, by Nagpa's* (male) or Nagma's* (female). These men and women often have taken the vows of the tantric tradition, without entering a monastery or convent. Being a Nagpa or Nagma is usually determined by lineage and is passed down in a family. As for these religious services Geoffrey Samuel points at two concepts: <u>Clerical Buddhism</u> that uses written texts as the source for its teachings, rituals and religious practices, and <u>Shamanic</u> or <u>Tantric Buddhism</u> that goes back to the oral tradition and is passed on through family trees, reincarnation* or the relation between teacher and student, either male or female.

Samuel notes that Buddhism and Bon are special, because in each one both forms are found complementing each other inside a single system (Samuel 1998, 3). The nuns of Redna Menling are at ease with both forms, but in every day life the oral tradition seems closer to their perception, as Sherap's story shows:

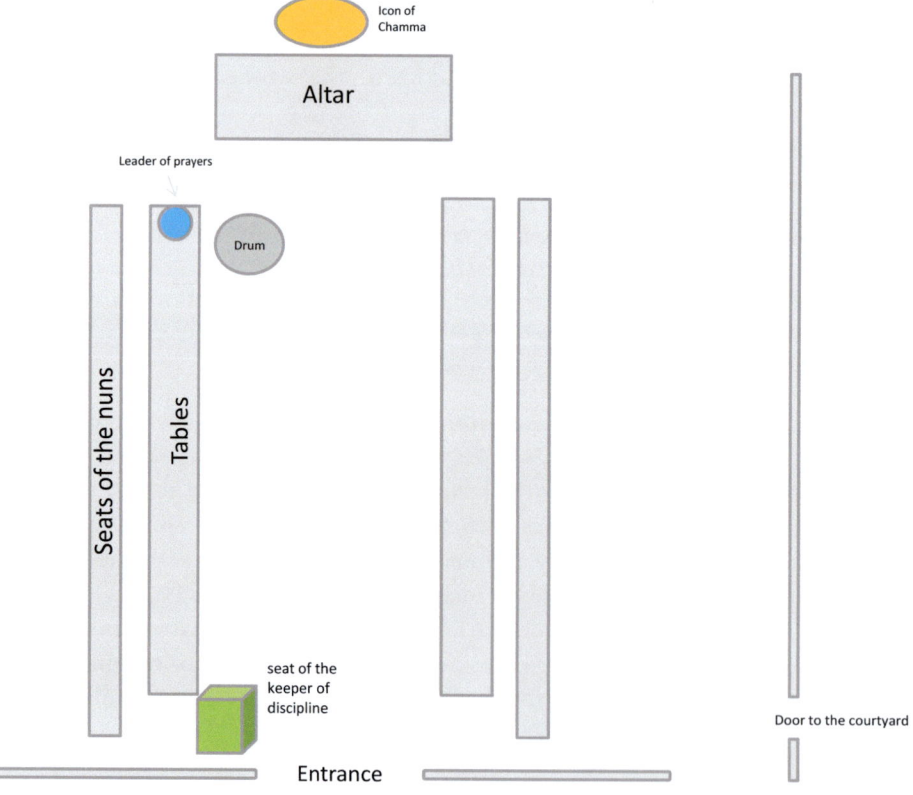

Figure 3.3: Plan of the temple of Redna Menling

Figure 3.4: The temple of Redna Menling

> *"In our family we pray often. It is more or less labrang, the house of a Lama. We do many rituals at home, when commemorating people. No, I have not been many times to the monastery or the temple."* [12]

A woman may have several reasons to enter a convent. A convent may have received custody over her as a young child, predestining the girl for a religious life. Or economic circumstances may have forced her to choose for a religious life. Redna Menling has been trusted with the care of 30 girls ranging from 4 to 14 years. A convent is a guarantee for a good education, but the mere fact that the girls spent their school years in a nunnery does not mean that they have to become a nun.

By the end of secondary school the girls themselves decide whether to take the vows. They also may profess later in life after fulfilling their obligations towards their family, for instance raising children. Such women often decide not to follow the long years of training required for the full investiture as a nun.

That brings up the next subject: why do the young women of Redna Menling choose a nun's life.

3.3 Connections between Biography and Motives to Profess

There is not one single reason why women do enter a convent. As said before, every story is unique and the circumstances are never the same. Yet there are similarities in the motives the women present for becoming a nun.

---

12   Interview, Ani Sherap Sangmo, 4 September 2007.

Three main motives bring continuity in the stories:
- A <u>practical choice</u> to enter a convent, mainly because it holds the promise of studying.
- The choice for a convent was inspired by <u>religious motives</u>.
- The choice imposed by the <u>political climate</u> in the country of origin.

3.3.1 Practical Considerations

All nuns mention the hard life of their mother as an important motive to choose for a life in a convent. It is striking how many times the extremely burdensome life of women is mentioned to explain this choice. Take for instance the story of Tsundu Sangmo:

> *"My sister was nineteen years old when she was surprised by a heavy snowstorm, while driving our herds in the fields. She died in that storm. My older sister died in childbirth. She was expecting twins and there were complications. There was no doctor in the vicinity. My mother died when I was three. She had the same problems as my sister, when pregnant. A woman's life is hard and difficult."* [13]

Or the story of Tsewang Tserap:

> *"The story of my mother? My mother had a very hard life. It is hard economically, there has to be food for everyone, and also you have to move in with another family when you marry. That is not an easy thing, especially not for girls. I would have been able to choose my own husband. My mother was not able to do that, her marriage was arranged."* [14]

That is how female life is experienced in the uplands of Nepal: hard and difficult. Caring for the children, arranged marriages, hard physical labour in the fields and lack of medical care.

Many women have to cope on their own, as the men are often busy, away from home. The women, whose choice for the convent was influenced by their mothers struggle in life, often admit that they find a nun's life an easy life.

Easy, because they only bear responsibility for themselves and are in a position to realise a better life. As a rule the death of a mother means that a daughter has to take over her role and responsibilities. And later, when a new woman enters the home, these stepdaughters don't have much choice. Tashi, 27 years old, tells her story:

> *"I must have been ten, when my mother died. Sherab, my brother was nine. He is a monk now, here in the monastery. When my mother died, I could no longer go to school. I had to look after my father. He was a good man. He didn't drink or so. We had land and cattle, so I had to do the housekeeping and look after my father. Some years ago he remarried, with a good woman. She is nice. You can't stay in the house when you are unmarried or a nun. In such a case it is better to go and study a bit, if you can. In that way you may become a good nun. My father*

---

13 Interview, Ani Tsundu Sangmo, 4 September 2007.
14 Interview, Ani Tsewang Sherap, 18 September 2007.

> *says that uneducated people are just like animals. So it is better to become a nun. I was 25 when I came here. My father was happy that I was going to be a nun. He is glad that I can study. He said that he cannot stop me and that life is better being a nun. But I had to study hard, he said."* [15]

Not all parents are as supportive as Tashi's father. Some nuns tell that they had kept their decision to enter the Dolanji monastery hidden from their family. They often ran off. First to Kathmandu, in order to apply for travel documents or to find others with whom to make the journey. Some women had decided to enter the convent, but found out that their families refused to let them go. To profess normally requires consent, the family has to approve that a man or a women enters a monastery. As a rule the approval is given in a small ceremony in the monastery. The most common reason for a family to deny approval is that the girl is needed in the house or in the fields. As soon as a new woman is introduced in the family to take over her position in the house, usually after marrying a brother or the father, the approval usually is given all the same.

The family situation, economic hardship and the demanding life of women are presented as important reasons to opt for a religious life. Religious grounds are presented as evidence. The story of Kunsang, 15 years old, underlines these motives:

> *"I've never been to school. I took care of the cattle, worked in the fields. In our village the oldest children help and the younger go to school. I have a brother and a sister. My brother is here in the monastery, his name is Yungdrung and my sister goes to school in our village. I was seven when my mother died. That is why I had to stay at home. But now there is a new woman. I don't want to work in the house or in the fields, I thought. I thought it would be better to become a nun. As a nun I may say prayers and wear a Lama's robe. I thought that nuns lead a happy life, a peaceful life; that nuns pray for others. That is why I wanted to be a nun."* [16]

3.3.2 Inspired by Religion

The second of the primary motives is of a more religious nature. The women picture scenes from their lives, or past lives, as reasons to profess. Most eye catching is Lobsang's story. Lobsang is twenty and graduated from secondary school in India. She has a Tibetan father, her mother is from India and she grew up in Kinnoor in a home where religion did not occupy a central place.

Together leafing through her picture books I see the early years of a normal schoolchild: school outings, a circle of friends with boys and girls. Yet ever since she started to speak Lobsang made clear that she wanted to be a nun. As she admits, much against the wishes of her parents:

---

15   Interview, Ani Tashi Tsomo, 25 September 2007.
16   Interview, Ani Kunsang Lhamo, 26 September 2007.

Portrait of Ani Kunsel Wangmo
Practical Considerations

Ani Kunsel was born 19 years ago in Tsarka, Nepal. She is the oldest of six children and attends school until 12. From that time on she helps her family in keeping clean the house, working in the fields and looking after the cattle. After three years she moves to Kathmandu, in order to return to school. On arrival she is deemed too old to go to school. To earn some money she stays in the city and finds work with a Tibetan family.

There are several monasteries in the region where she grew up, and even as a child she thought about becoming a nun. Her mother is a Bonpo; her father a Buddhist. That leaves her a choice. One of her brothers chooses to become a monk in Dharamsala. She is very clear about her reasons for choosing a religious life in a nunnery:

"I wanted to become a nun because I have seen the life my mother lived. Life is not easy, when you have children. We were with six children at home. Some have an easygoing character; some have not. And then, a mother always worries. She cares for her children and has to work in the fields. My father was not at home much; he was often away, on business. A small kind of business. So my mother was often alone, We had relatives in the village. An aunt, who also had six children, died. She was my mothers' younger sister. The children were left alone. My mother sometimes helped the family, because the father had no one to help him. But she also had to take care of her own children."

Her parents support her choice:

"After I had decided to become a nun, someone took me here, with the money I had earned that year. Rinpoche received me and I said to him that I wanted to be a nun. Rinpoche asked: Can you be a nun. What did you do that year in Kathmandu? Why didn't you enter the convent in Kathmandu? I said to him that I would like to enter the convent here because I come from a Bon family. Then he said that he approved and that I would be a good nun. I put on the robe, took the vows and shaved my head. That was a kind of odd feeling. I had not felt that way before, but it made me glad."

Kunsel sees al kinds of prospects in being a nun. "Being a nun means that I can study. I may become someone with a good education, so that I might help my family. I would like the other children to go to school." When asked how she would support her family financially, as nuns do not earn money, after all, she turns out to have ideas of her own. "Right know I am learning to paint, to paint Thangkas. I think that when I am really good at it, I might sell them." This view brings about quite some turbulence; as such an idea is way beyond reality.

Kunsel likes being in Redna Menling where life comes with ease. *"I have classes where I learn to paint Thangkas, I do ring the bell, and I am the Chopon, that is the one arranging the offerings. I like doing that, it means that I do not have to cook or clean the kitchen."*

"I don't really know why women would want to become a nun. But some are very poor, for instance, and are looking for a way out. Then they become a nun. Nuns should help other people. You can pray, so that others may have a happy life. That also goes for monks, but monks have their own school and they can study very much and very long. If they are really dedicated, they may become a lama, or pass the Geshe exam. I wish that we also could do that."

When I ask Kunsel whether she knows that there are female Lama's in Tibet, she looks at me in doubt. As if she doesn't believe me. Then she asks Tashi, the interpreter, whether it is true. When Tashi says that it is true, her disbelief only seems to grow.

"Even as a child I wanted to be a nun. Whenever I saw someone in a robe, I wanted to wear one too. Monks and nuns were happy, I thought. My three sisters and my brother go to school, just like I did. Every time I asked if I could go to a convent, my father and mother said it was not possible. They refused. But I could not accept that. I asked it all the time, and every time they refused. First I had to finish my school. My parents thought I wouldn't be a good nun, for I was a very naughty child, often harassing other children. I was a little worried about that too, but I knew exactly what I wanted, I wanted to be a nun. There is a nun in our village, Ani Moni. She is about 55. I often visited her. I was eight the first time I went to see her."

Actually I didn't know at all that nuns have to learn so many things. But when I came to visit the nunnery I grew even more enthusiastic. I was fascinated by the discipline and by speaking Tibetan. I think that in a past live I was a Tibetan. After passing my school exams I said to my mother that I would go, but still my mother refused her consent. But when my mother was away for work, my father agreed. My mother did not and still does not. Every time she asks me to come home, but I cannot and I don't want to.

When I came here Rinpoche did not agree right away. He, and the other members of the commission thought it would be very hard for me to get used to the life of a nun. I had been to a mixed school and had had a normal life. They all thought that I was not serious. But I was. Some months later I went again to Rinpoche to ask him to accept me on further consideration. I said that I was able to keep my vows, for that is why they hesitated. The convent accepted me. I felt I had to stay here in this convent, a Bon convent, even though I do not come from a Bon family." [17]

While I am in Dolanji Lobsang's father comes to visit her. I managed to meet him. He takes pride in his daughter, though he still finds it hard to accept her choice to be a nun. But it is as he said: *"It is a mystery, but ever since she could talk she said that she was going to be a nun. I have to accept that."*

3.3.3 A Choice Forced by Political Reality

Not all women were free to choose shelter in a monastery. At first talking about their motives with some of the nuns was hampering. They shared many things, but something in their stories didn't add up. Then one nun mentioned problems with Maoists militants in the region she came from. It was a shocking story. Maoist groups invading villages to seize and abduct young children to be trained as a soldier. The villagers tried to find safe havens for their children and among others they turned to the monasteries in India, where the children could attend school. In 2007 the organisation Human Rights Watch published a survey of the way the Maoist militants in Nepal abduct children in order to turn them into soldiers.

---

17   Interview, Ani Lobsang Wangmo, 6 September 2007.

Portrait of Ani Monlam Sangmo
Inspired by Religion

Ani Monlam Sangmo, 23 years old, was born and bred in a Buddhist family in Kinnoor, India. The farming family had five children, three girls and two boys. Monlam is still young, when her father dies in a car accident.

She goes to school but leaves in the second year, after losing much time due to health problems: *"I suffered from a sort of seizures; I couldn't stand on my legs. It is something unclean, being possessed by spirits. That is what is said in Tibet. A Lama treated and healed me. This Lama then advised me to become a nun. He said it was better for me to be a nun."*

At 18 she decides to follow the Lama's advice and enters the Redna Menling convent. It is a day's travel from her native region. The fact that she doesn't have to pay a contribution, as is common in Buddhist monasteries, prompts the choice for the specific (Bon) convent. What's more, Monlam can easily travel home from Dolanji, in case her mother would fall ill.

"I do not come from a Bon family, but this convent is close to my home, in case problems should arise there. I grew up in a very religious family; I am not like the other nuns. My mother was with me, when the Lama told me that it would be better for me to become a nun. But in the end I made that choice myself. My mother gave me leave to go. I came here on my own credence and because of what the Lama said. When I became a nun I expected life to be good. Rinpoche takes care of all; he cares for all, from the head to the toes. For me that is a good life."

She tells how a Geshe from Kinnoor escorted her to His Holiness, to be admitted to the convent:

"A Geshe from Kinnoor was also there. He has a good reputation. He was a kind of sponsor, like a mediator. Fourteen or fifteen other people were present, not monks but laymen. They came to testify for me. They testified that I would not go home. That is what they said."

Monlam is satisfied with her life as a nun, she feels she does important work: *"When people are ill they go to a Lama, or to someone else who is a religious person. Then prayers are said on behalf of them. That is important. Those are the things we are learning to do. During the day we practise the prayers for Chamma, in the evening the prayers for Chod*."*

She is quite clear about the differences in the monasterial tradition between men and women: *"I don't believe there are differences between monks and nuns, apart from the classes. For the monks there are Lama's and several teachers, we have only one teacher. As nuns we sit all together in one class, it would be better if we had different classes. It would be much easier then to see whether a nun makes good progress. It would be a good thing when a monk or a Lama would teach us how to handle ritual instruments, like the drums and that sort of things. I don't think it matters whether the teacher is a man or a woman, what matters is a person's heart. If someone stays pure, is pure in his or her heart, then there is no difference between men and women."*

She has a critical eye on her fellow-nuns. *"Some of them hang pictures of artists and such things on the wall. I don't like that. For me Tonpa Sherab is the most important. When something happens, or when I need something, I say Tonpa Sherab, Tonpa Sherab . . ."*

As far as the future is concerned, both her own and of the other nuns: *"I don't know whether there will be a female spiritual leader in the times to come. Right now the most important person in the Bon is Menri Rinpoche. But as for the future, I don't know.*

I think I have to stay pure in my heart and have to study hard, so that I have a good education. I want to stay here in the convent and serve the convent. When you are a nun you are always happy and it is impossible to be not satisfied."

"Most of the children we interviewed said that the Maoists took them from their homes for what they said would be a short-term participation in a 'campaign', a period of a month or two. But when the children tried to leave after the initial 'campaign' period was over, the Maoists would not let them go, or would recapture them if they escaped"

(Human Rights Watch 2007).

The information from the report opened the possibility to talk with the girls and women about what happened in the region they come from. The result was a series of curdling stories. Because the Maoists try to take children, both boys and girls, from 12 to 16 years, many parents give their children in this age in the care of monks, who have promised to bring them to India and make sure that they go to school. Once in the monastery in India it often turns out that education is no longer an option. Many of these children have had very little education and there is no chance to recover these arrears. To find a solution the girls I interviewed were taken to a convent where they took their vows.

Yangzo tells what happened to her:

"There were many problems. Especially at night there were many problems. The Maoists came at night, but in other villages also in during the day. They said they were going to take one child from every family. And they have taken a child from almost every family. My brother was send to the city, so that they couldn't take him. I was send here, because I am rather tall for my age. And you never know, with Maoists. Now we have only two children left at home. They will not take them, they are safe. The Maoists might even have taken me if I had gone to school. You must go away, far away. When I came here I was told I was too old to go to school. That is why I was left behind here in the convent. One day I was given the robe and my hair was shaved. I miss my family, but we write each other. Sometimes I get letters." [18]

Yangzo's story is the story of a group of young nuns who arrived in Dolanji in 2004, driven by the political climate in Nepal. Most of these girls were not raised in a very religious place, and none of them is from a Bon family. They all try to bring their expectations in line with the situation they have landed in. Sometimes that calls for an outlook on life that is hard to uphold.

This pain sometimes is found in the stories, for instance in what 16-year-old Tender went through. She arrived in Dolanji when she was 13:

"We had hard times with the Maoists. It was very dangerous in the village where I lived. Many families fled to Humla, a big city close by. My parents told me to go with a monk, Yung. Yung said that the oldest children would go to a monastery and the young ones to school. But when I came here, all the girls I knew went to the convent, I was left alone at school. I felt sad. I don't know how to tell this.

---

18 Interview, Ani Lobsang Wangmo, 6 September 2007.

Portrait of Ani Yangzo Dolmo
A choice forced by political reality

17-Year old Yangzo Dolmo is born in the little village of Dangshy, Nepal, in a family with four children. She goes to school but when she turns 12 she has to stay home to help her mother. In the interview she initially suggests that her choice to become a nun is inspired by her aunt, who is a nun: *"My father's sister is a nun and I have seen how she lives. That is what I wanted for myself. Family life is hard, especially when you are a mother with many children. Being a nun you only have to take care of yourself, not of anyone else. . . . I was still young. My father told me that I was too young but an uncle from my mother's side said that it is good to become a nun, even when you are young. My mother thought it was a good idea for me to go to the convent. . . . Being a nun is a happy life. My mother had some influence, but becoming a nun was a decision I made myself. I am happy and content being a nun. I never thought of getting married."*

But when I bring up the Maoist militants, the urge to become a nun turns out to be determined by other factors as well: *"There were many problems, mostly at night. They [the Maoists] said they were going to take one child from every family. And they have taken a child from almost every family. They came to us in the night, but hadn't taken children yet. It is because of these problems that we are here now. . . . We were scared, very scared . . . . My brother was sent to the city, where the Maoists can't take him. And I was sent here. Now there are only two children left at home. They don't take the little ones, they are safe. When I came here they said I was to old to go to school again. The little ones go to school, but I was left behind here, in the convent."*

Telling this, she can't hold back her emotions. When I ask how it feels to be a nun, she says: *I don't want to say anything about this question. I don't know an answer. I am content with the life I have known."*

Yangzo travelled from Nepal to Dolanji with a large group of children. Because the abbot isn't there when they reached Dolanji, the group has to wait some days in the village.

"When we arrived, we cut off our hair. But they were not allowed to wear the robe yet, that had to wait until Rinpoche returned. You cannot cut off you hair and wear normal clothes. That is why we only wore our yellow underwear . . . . I knew why they cut off my hair; I knew I was going to be a nun. Rinpoche came after two days, and then we took our vows. I don't remember what I promised. That was the day I was given my robe."

She tries to find her way in the nunnery of Redna Menling, in her nun's life: *"Being a nun you have to have to do your studies, you have to have a good heart and to be nice to other persons. You must behave well in the group, and not fight. There isn't so much fighting anymore and not so much quarrelling. But it has not been like that all the time."*

She does see differences between monks and nuns, in particular where the level of training is concerned and where that leads to later on. *"There are differences between monks and nuns. We don't have to spend money; the monks have to pay for everything themselves. It would be hard if we had to pay too. Unless you have parents who can send you money. The monks earn money by saying prayers. We don't get money when we say prayers. We get pocket money on special days, but not for saying prayers. The monks can also study to become a Geshe. We can't, though I would like to do it. "*

When talking about the future, she returns to the example set by her aunt the nun: *"For later I want to be like my aunt. I want to study well and have a pure heart."*

Then I said I too wanted to become a nun. I didn't want to be alone. Now I am a nun, and maybe that is also good. I want to be healthy and happy. Maybe later I can go and travel." [19]

These kinds of events turn Redna Menling into an asylum, apart from being a convent.

From the stories and the quotes given here, three groups of nuns can be distinguished: those who are religiously inspired, those who have personal reasons to profess and those who sought a safe place in a convent from political turmoil. Often it is impossible to draw clear dividing lines between these groups. Personal reasons, such as seeking an opportunity to study, may intermingle with religious motives belonging to the cultural background of the women.

Religious merit holds a central place in the Bon tradition. The merit may be granted through a system of reciprocity. For instance by giving donations to a monastery, or to an individual monk, nun, or Lama or to a religious authority. But a nun, monk or any other person who is religiously active also gathers merits by saying prayers or performing rituals in exchange for donations. This is also the leading principle where reincarnation is concerned: gathering merits helps to make a future life better than the present one. Saying prayers, doing good deeds, bestowing gifts have a positive influence. Choosing a life as a nun is a deed of merit, as the aura of good merit doesn't only shine for you but also brings merit to your next of kin in this life and in lives to come. Regarding the very limited space the women have to make their choices, a nun's life brings good merit from a religious point of view.

3.4 The Ties between Daily Life and the Expectations of Life as a Nun

The young women have ideas about life after entering the convent, but are these expectations matched by reality? What impact do the expectations have on the day-by-day reality they live as nuns? As this step is decisive, I dwell upon the transition from secular life to a religious life inside the walls of the convent.

Entering the convent may be seen as a rite of passage (Turner 1969). On becoming a nun a women steps out of their secular life and starts a new, religious life, a transition marked by rituals.

That calls for the presence of witnesses at the moment the nun-to-be takes her vows. The witnesses are there to testify that the family of the woman accepts that she professes and that her motives are pure. They testify that there is nothing that can prevent her becoming a nun. Prior to the ceremony the nun, or someone else, cuts her hair. From that moment on she will wear nothing but the garments of the convent. The androgynous appearance of the nun after cutting her hair is enhanced by the fact that monks and nuns wear the same robes. The family name makes way for a religious name, given by the person who administers the vows and afterwards the nun is always addressed as Ani. The women declare that the cutting

---

19 Interview, Ani Tender Wangmo, September 2007.

of their hair for them was the most impressing moment. I was struck by the fact that none of the nuns mentioned the moment of receiving their new name, unless I asked about it specifically.

In *The Rites of Passage* Arnold van Gennep bestows special significance on the cutting of the hairs. He calls it a watershed, separating secular life from religious life:

> *"To cut the hair is to separate oneself from the previous world: to dedicate the hair is to bind oneself to the sacred world ..."* (Gennep 1960, 166).

For the women of Redna Menling cutting their hair symbolised the vow to dedicate their lives to the Bon, or as one of the nuns said, 'dedicating you to Tonpa Sherab and to fulfilling religious obligations'.

The women and girls all have their own story, when it comes to the cutting of their hair. For some of them it was a climax, the confirmation of their choice. For others it was a shock, whether they had made a positive choice for the convent or not. Some say they had to get used to it and that it was a weird feeling. One of the young girls cried, when she recalled the moment her hair was cut off.

This is how Kunsel remembers the moment she lost her hair:

> *"It was a weird feeling when my hair was cut off, I couldn't get used to it. When I arrived here, my hair was very long. I had beautiful hair. But that is part of the deal, when you want to be a nun."* [20]

A woman's hair is considered a jewel in the Tibetan community. It is well tended, brushed and combed and oiled. On special occasions a woman may wear precious stones in her hair, and the various hairstyles indicate whether she is married or still available for marriage. Cutting off the hair signals that a woman is no longer available for marriage. It also means that she renounces motherhood, celibacy is one of the most important vows she takes.

Van Gennep (1960) and Turner (1969) found that rituals meant to confirm these transitions mark important phases in human life. Turner sees these rituals as a process, characterized by three stages: *separation, liminality and reintegration.*

Untying or removal from the normal daily structure signifies separation: a physical separation. Untying, or being removed brings about a situation characterised by liminality. In Turners view that is a so-called anti-structure in which nothing is anymore what it used to be. Roles and identities one believed one could rely on dissipate (in the case of Redna Menling, the secular life the women had). Individuals end up in a state of ambiguity.

Turner sees this liminal state as the most important phase in the process. He calls it *betwixt and between* (Turner 1969, 95), the state in which a person is neither this nor that. In Turners view persons in a liminal phase do not fit in in the regular classifications used for a cultural setting.

Women entering a convent, for whatever reason, are turned into a nun through a ceremony. That is the starting point of a life that is very much unlike the life they had been leading so far. Perhaps even more important is that taking the vows

---

20 Interview, Ani Kunsel Wangmo, 20 September 2007.

changes them into a novice; not a layperson anymore, but not yet a full-fledged nun. This is the liminal phase, as defined by Victor Turner.

On entering the convent the basic vows are taken. More vows are taken in the following years, depending on her development as a nun and her personal needs and wishes. Children given into the care of the convent usually take their vows about the age of 18. The choice is immanent when graduating from secondary school: do they want to stay in the convent or do they prefer a secular life. Time and again I was assured that the children are free to choose. Not all of them crave a life as a nun, even though they spent most of their years in the nunnery. The vows are not taken, unless the woman has a clear view of their meaning and consequences. Everyone has the right to suspend the vows for a certain time, when doubts arise or when circumstances force a nun or monk to renounce religious life temporarily. During my stay in Dolanji I have met two monks who had suspended their vows, to renew them after a certain period. Their motives were not revealed.

A monastic tradition focuses on study, on passing on knowledge by means of written texts. For most girls and women, however, reading and writing poses a serious problem, as only a minority has enjoyed any education. In view of that reality, it is striking that all nuns, without exemption, mention access to studying as a prime motive. Tashi, 27 years and never been to school in Nepal, tells:

> *"When you are smart it is easy to study, but when you are not it is hard. Long time ago, when I was still at home, I very much wanted to be able to study. But it was impossible. I had to look after my father and run the house. Now at last I have the opportunity. I have to learn to read and write and whenever I have some time off I do extra exercises in writing. I have to begin with the alphabet and that is not an easy thing. But my brother told me that is always hard in the beginning and that it will be easier in due time if I do my best. I had a hard time getting used to studying, because I never went to school at all and I didn't know how to start. When I was asked something, I started to tremble all over and couldn't remember anything anymore. But once I have learned to read and write, I can learn other things. Now I'm always afraid that I do not know the right answer to a question."* [21]

Every day in a monastery has a fixed rhythm, setting a strict agenda in which (self)study and temple meetings take a leading place. Redna Menling is a new convent, before the nuns could begin their training most of them had to learn to read and write Tibetan. Moreover the extensive construction work was still going on, and building activities still are part of the daily program: cutting rocks, hauling stones and all preparatory work for the new buildings normally are done by the nuns themselves. Most of them find it a welcome break, though not when it must be done for days on end. Namdak. 22 and living in the convent since 2006, gives an accurate description of a 'normal' day in the convent:

---

21 Interview, Ani Tashi Tsomo, 25 September 2007.

> "Usually I get up at five o'clock, but that is different for everyone. I start studying at five, but if it comes easy, you don't have to get up that early. We gather in the temple at seven and pray together until eight. Then we have breakfast. The nuns who prepare the meals don't have to come to the temple. Between eight and half past eight the teacher arrives. The classes go on until noon. Then we assemble in the temple and have lunch. After lunch we have time off until three o'clock. I need that time to do my laundry, arrange my room and take a shower. Sometimes, when I am not tired I try to practice some writing. We are all new so we have to learn everything from the start. Sometimes we have to sit apart with a group that has just arrived to practice Tibetan. At three o'clock we say prayers and have tea in the temple. After that we have classes until about six, dinner time. I am learning now to play the big trumpet, so I have to practice in the evening. Usually we are free one day in the week. That gives us also time to practice."[22]

The programme is the same for all nuns, but some have special or extra duties. Those who have kitchen duty or who are ill don't have to come to the temple for the regular gatherings.

Most nuns of Redna Menling have next of kin, mostly male, who have entered the monastery. Their experiences colour the expectations of the nuns: a clean life, filled with study, ample time and opportunity to pray for a better next life for themselves, their next of kin and people they know. Being a nun they only have themselves to look after, and there is nothing to look forward to, nothing to look back at. Marriages hold more uncertainties, as one never knows what a husband and children will bring. These were in general the answers to questions about life's expectations.

As a rule the nuns find life in the convent easy, except for the learning they have to do. There are some exceptions: a few young girls who didn't come out of free will, and Lobsang who never had to help out at home.

This is how Rinchen describes the relatively easy life in the convent:

> "I am the Leader of Discipline in the temple. That means that I have to make sure that everything happens neatly according the rules. I learned how to lead the prayers and I have done that for three years. I don't have to cook and I am free from household jobs. For me there is nothing difficult here, apart from the writing exercises. That I find hard. The spelling of Tibetan is very difficult. But I am happy, life is smooth, the convent gives us all we need, such as shelter, clothing and food and there is no reason for worrying. When I compare this with life in my village in Nepal, this is really an easy life and I am very happy with it."[23]

When sitting and talking with the nuns, many refer to the troubles that used to be in the nunnery. A group of nuns has returned to Nepal. Some of them went to Kathmandu where there is a group of nuns living close to a Bon monastery, others returned home.

---

22   Interview, Ani Namdak Lhamo, 26 September 2007.
23   Interview, Ani Rinchen Sangmo, 5 September 2007.

Figure 3.5 and figure 3.6: Studying nuns

The problems may have sprung from the different circumstances under which the women entered the convent. Monlam remembers the troubles:

> *"Some did run away or wanted to do so. They wanted to return home. A convent needs discipline. Good discipline is important. When one or two women leave, that puts shame on the others. It puts them in an awkward position. Other people may think we are all that way, but that is not so. Everyone has her own way of thinking. I think that has to do with the problems."* [24]

---

24   Interview, Ani Monlam Sangmo, 20 September 2007.

Figure 3.7 and figure 3.8: Working nuns

These words do not unveil the exact background of the problems, but it is clear that it all had to do with failing to live up to expectations. It was all about a group of very young Nepalese girls, who because of political circumstances had sought refuge in the convent.

I have already mentioned the daily routines, dictated by study, work and fulfilling religious duties. Though that rhythm forms the backbone of the programme in the convent, as a community of nuns the young women have a hard time finding a structure of their own. This can partly be explained by the diverging interests of the different groups inside the nunnery. Unless they have made the choice for the convent themselves, religious duties do not come first, while for the women who made that choice consciously these duties represent the essence of their life. Conflicting interests and concerns do not bring about a close knit community. Debates and arguments about wearing t-shirts with prints under the robes (formally not allowed) and the number of hours allowed for watching television, are persistent. Because all women are still in training and none of them is really familiar with all aspects of monasterial life, there isn't anyone in a position to lead the convent and solve the daily recurring disagreements.

As a rule a monastery is led by an abbot, or in case of a convent, an abbess. In Tibet most convents are built close to a men's monastery, and often the abbot of the monastery also leads the convent. This is the case in Redna Menling, where none of the nuns is in a position to claim daily responsibility. There is no balance in the relations between the groups inside the convent and among the nuns there isn't anyone with sufficient authority, based on age or experience, to assume daily leadership. One of its effects is that in particular the young girls given in care of the convent, feel lost and sometimes unprotected. The absence of daily leadership inside the group makes some young nuns feel insecure and lonely. Living in a convent demands a great deal of adaptation, especially from girls who did not make that choice themselves.

The programme of studies is supervised by a Lama is identical for all nuns. The decision to give relatively new nuns extra support in learning to read and write Tibetan, gives rise to resentment and irritation among other nuns. Some have entered the convent earlier and want to avoid unnecessary repetition, others just want to study faster. I have addressed this problem in the meetings I had with the abbot, because I had the impression that at whiles Redna Menling seems to be lacking a steady course and that setting up a sound education scheme doesn't have any priority.

The abbot partly acknowledges these problems and regrets the absence of a woman capable of taking over daily control. As for the teaching programme, he indicated that plans for improving the curriculum will have to wait, because in astrological terms this is the Year of the Rat. The abbot explained that in such a year it is not advisable to introduce serious changes.

It is striking that some of the monks I interviewed denied this. Some Geshes bluntly say they would choose a different approach: a more detailed curriculum, a programme aiming to train the nuns in managing the daily affairs of the convent themselves, so that in due time nuns may indeed lead the convent. Geshe Samdup, director of the Zhan-Bod Documentation Center, presents the following proposition:

> *"These times do need convents. It is apparent that interest is growing, that more women are ready to profess. It is important however that we offer them a sound education and that they learn how to lead a community. That would end the need for men to mingle with a nunnery. In my view women should be self-sufficient as far as their convent is concerned, which also means that for now we should go on supporting them. It is in that field, that there are problems now, developments go*

too slow. They, I mean the nuns, do not get enough lessons. If His Holiness were to ask me what we should do, I would say: make sure that two or three monks are available every day for teaching religious classes and see to it some of the nuns receive training in all that is needed to run a community, the financial side included. It is my dream that the nuns can do everything themselves." [25]

Some nuns frankly voice their hope that the years to come will bring a more varied educational programme and that the classes will be led by women.

Blending a community harbouring so many different motives while monastic life is not supported by long years of experience and tradition, is not an easy task. But the women do have in common a religious praxis to which they dedicate their life as a nun.

3.4.1 Theoretical Intermezzo: Communitas

Victor Turner distinguishes four different forms of *communitas*, springing from the process of a *Rite of Passage* during the liminal phase. Turner argues that from the state of liminality emerges a form of *communitas*, a way of being together that appears when mutual differences between individuals disappear. Turner lists three kinds of *communitas*:

1. Existential or spontaneous communitas; this form doesn't require a social structure.
2. Normative communitas, that comes about when liminality endures and develops a social structure within its boundaries.
3. Ideological communitas, that refers to a form of community which reveals itself as an ideal form of being together. (Turner 1969, 132)

In spite of their mutual differences and diverse motives all the nuns of Redna Menling are in more or less the same position: they form a community, whether they like it or not. Even if an individual nun does not feel a really integrated, the outer world does see her as a member of the community and addresses her as such. It is essential, as Turner appropriately remarks, that it remains apparent that each community, each *communitas*, consists of relations between individuals who each have their own background and history (Turner 1969, 131).

From that angle one might say that the nuns of Redna Menling form a normative *communitas*. Inside the group the women may develop individually, each according her own talents, wishes and expectations, but also with the ability to adapt to the situation they are part of. In doing so, a feeling of belonging arises, that stems from a steady structure, in this case the vows each woman has taken on entering the convent.

---

25 Interview, Geshe Shenphen Samdup, 20 August 2007.

This mechanism is highlighted in the following fragment from the interview with 19 year old Ani Metok Sangmo. Her parents sent her to Dolanji, intending to protect her from Maoist attacks on her village. On arriving in Dolanji she did not realise she was going to be a nun:

"In my daily life everything is easy. I have a big responsibility towards the group, because I am the Treasurer, the controller. Later I want to practise and to study. I do not want to go home. I want to study well and become a 'well-know' person. I want to become a well educated person. Right now it is not possible to become a Geshe, but maybe later I can." [26]

Metok found a strategy to adapt to the situation she is in, from a girl she turned into a nun. In a set structure the liminal situation offers the possibility to develop oneself, to define and identify oneself. In the exchange with this society her personality grows and adapts itself, making it possible for Metok to develop from a girl to a nun.

This is what Erikson (1968) calls 'ego-identity', a development leading to the expansion of the abilities which make up the link between acquiring a skill and its cultural meaning. Without exemption the nuns say that the possibility to study was one of the most important reasons to profess. Going to school, and graduating at the end of it, brings a person a high social status in the world they grew up in. The possibility to link one's situation with something of 'value' gives meaning to that situation.

From such a condition grows a feeling of self-esteem, developing step by step towards confidence that the ego is capable of effective measures. An ego develops in connection with social reality and tries to integrate it so that a person may grow to be a well organised ego in a social reality (Erikson 1968, 48-49).

Metok's social reality is the convent, but before that it was the Nepalese society where she grew up. To study, or to have studied has a special meaning for Metok. It refers to persons who hold a special status in society. Being a good nun is important for Metok. In that way she complies with the values and standards held by others in relation to life in the convent. By underlining the implication of education she contributes to important values and standards. Developing an identity corresponds with being important to somebody else and it is essential that this identity is confirmed by persons you personally respect.

Metok has succeeded in transforming the evolution of her identity into a positive process of adaptation. In spite of feelings of danger and insecurity, imposed by what happened in Nepal, she managed to find her place in the collective of the convent. The fact that some of the nuns have left, shows that a process like this doesn't always have a positive outcome.

But also a 'we-feeling' can be found in the position of the convent towards the monastery of the men. The men always know better, have had a better education, and as a group the nuns strive to equal that standard. In addition, it provokes a strong feeling of being different, of being a woman.

---

26 Interview, Ani Metok Sangmo, 5 September 2007.

This feeling of 'we' and 'them', the gender difference, and the difference in education strengthens the feeling of normative *communitas* among the nuns. They form a community inside the greater community of the Menri Monastery.

In the next chapter I will discuss how the relative new community of nuns, harbouring many different backgrounds, and the much larger Menri community relate to each other.

Chapter 4

The community of nuns | Interaction with its surroundings

4.1 Religious Praxis and Integration in Daily Life

Individual motives, as well as circumstances and backgrounds, moved young women to enter a monastery. The interaction between these individual motives and backgrounds prompted a monasterial community. What does this individual path of each woman contribute to life in a religious community? What is the influence of this young monasterial community on the so much larger religious community of Menri? And what influences from the outside world, are working on the Bon community?

In the monasterial community (a normative *communitas*) study and practising the religious praxis take a central place. Using the religious practise I will in this fourth chapter provide an insight in the positions of the nuns, their relation with the community of religious men, with the community of laypersons and with influences from outside the Bon.

Gender relations and ideas about the body and physicality take an important place in the exchange between praxis, community and outside influences. Relying on the theoretical notes on *Grid* and *Group* of Mary Douglas and by applying Rita Gross' insights on gender questions in Buddhism, I want to connect the monasterial life as perceived by the nuns of Redna Menling with the way they interact with their surroundings.

As the religious praxis forms the core of monasterial life in Redna Menling, it is evident that first insight must be given in its aims and functions.

4.1.1 The Aim of Religious Praxis

Performing religious praxis is the cornerstone of monasterial life. Directly or indirectly, this praxis focuses on the community. For some reason a layperson asks the religious community, or one of its members, to do certain rituals or services. It may concern prayers for a sick person, or rituals for a deceased to ensure a genial reincarnation. Rituals are done either in the temple or in a private home. Even rituals which are initiated by the religious community often have a link with the lay community, as many rituals honour gods or goddesses or beg for something beneficial for the entire community.

In return for the religious services the monastery or the religious person involved receives a payment in cash or goods. This reciprocity is rooted in an age-old tradition that for centuries kept a social, economic and religious balance in the Tibetan uplands. Another tradition is the custom that monks and nuns are financially supported by their family. Having a next of kin who has taken the vows is considered an honour and a merit. It brings better hope of advancing to an improved new life and has a positive effect on the whole family. Being a community in exile in India, the ties between the Bon community and the family and the lay community have lost a part of the obviousness they had in Tibet. It is now essential to find new ways to support the religiously active community.

The aim of the individual practice is to find redemption from the cycle of samsara*, the eternal cycle of birth, death and rebirth. This is achieved through meditation, special exercises and secret teachings, involving a special relation between teacher and devotee.

Though not openly discussed, the ranking of a ritual is linked to the person carrying it out. Lineage, certain reincarnations, special talents, a special teacher or social esteem determine the value attributed to the performing of a ritual. Women in general, and the nuns of Redna Menling in particular, lack the backing of lineage or reincarnation. Such a reality determines the place or social status they hold in the eyes of the lay community.

Before sketching where this may lead to, I will give an outline of the everyday routine, a seen by the nuns themselves. Monlam is to give her view on religious life:

> *"The day we take our vows, we promise not to kill anymore, not to say bad things about somebody else; all these things we have to keep in our heart and think about them again and again. From that day on we have to tell ourselves not to do bad things. On the day you receive the robe, you must realise that it is the robe of the Buddha, and that we should be happy to receive it. Being a nun you must be aware of all the things that come with wearing the robe. It is the simple life of a nun; your spoon, your bowl should be made of wood.*
>
> *We must help our families to avoid ending up in hell in a next life, and the only things that can help are the good merits we have gathered. I say all prayers to remove obstacles on this path. I do that for my family, for other people, for Rinpoche in particular, but also for the people who sponsor me. I do it, so that they may get a better life than they have now. Maybe they are happy, in that case they have a chance of an even better life."* [27]

Monlam is one of the nuns who are longest in Dolanji. She arrived in 2001, before Redna Menling was built. Going to class, the daily services for Chamma in the temple, doing Kor-Ra's and numerous times reciting individual prayers together form her daily religious praxis. Apart from the daily prayers and rituals, such as the sang* ritual in the morning - which is a fire-and-smoke offering to purify the surroundings and conciliate the gods and goddesses - there are special prayers and rituals requested by villagers and visitors of the monastery. The daily reality is that the rituals done for the laymen often falter. One of the reasons is that the nuns of Redna Menling have not yet mastered all rituals and in certain

---

27   Interview, Ani Monlam Wangmo, 6 September 2007.

cases they shouldn't even be asked to do them. For instance, in the three months of my research villagers hardly ever trusted the nunnery to perform rituals, not even the rituals they have mastered. The monks, on the other hand, are often asked to do rituals. When the nuns are set to work, it usually are the women of the village, asking for a certain ritual of prayer. These requests are neatly noted in a book. The Lama appoints the tasks and names the nuns to say these prayers in the temple. A record is held of all payments and by the end of the year the scores are settled with the monks of the Menri Monastery. The nunnery decides how to spend a part of the money. This is done under responsibility of the Treasurer. When I had to leave for America, I asked the nuns to pray for a safe trip and donated a sum directly to the convent. This led to utter confusion. The destination of the money was discussed agitatedly. The contrast with the way the monks deal with such an event is great. Monks are paid individually to say prayers and do rituals. They don't have to explain what they use the money for. The community of monks performs rituals in the temple all the time, in line with the ritual calendar. While I was in Dolanji I witnessed a large procession to celebrate the full moon ritual. The nuns did not participate, all we could do was to climb up to the roof and watch the proceedings.

It is evident that the villagers frequently call for the assistance of the community of monks, and contribute financially to the rituals held in the temple of the monks. And when there is an important ritual in the main temple, a sign outside the entrance lists the amounts people have donated for the event. It appears the villagers have more confidence in the monks than in the nuns, when it comes to rituals. This gives rise to grumbling among the nuns. *"They get paid and they don't pay us, even when we are asked to say certain prayers"*, is a common complaint.

Halfway through October a man from Tibet and his sister paid a visit to the monastery. The man and the woman came to see the nunnery and asked the nuns to do a ritual for them in the temple. It is the first time I watched the very impressing Chod ritual. The ritual is not only meant for the nuns to practice, they also will perform it when asked to. Later it became evident that the family has really paid generously, boosting the self-esteem of the nuns. By the end of September His Holiness left for America for a few months. This prompted the nuns to start reciting prayers six days long, asking for the removal of hindrances on the way and for a safe arrival in the USA. When the Dalai Lama went to New York to receive an important award out of the hands of the president of the USA, the nuns kept the fire of offerings burning all day and did a ceremony of blessing in the temple.

As Monlam said before in the quoted fragment about her praxis, she also prays for her sponsors. The external sponsors have partly taken over the function the neighbouring village used to have. Geshe Samdup affirms that it is popular nowadays the support women's projects:

> *"The convent is growing so fast because it offer good facilities. We have many people who take an interest and support it. And of course people are interested in new developments. As we say, nuns form a 'trend'. Maybe people are getting used to monks and like something new, like women becoming monks. That is why so many people are interested."* [28]

It is a common complaint among monks that it is relatively easy to raise funds for women and children. Many foreign organisations have links with certain Geshes or His Holiness. During visits to countries in the West religious teaching is often combined with raising money for projects run by the Geshes, such as amenities for children. Apart from that, there is a system operating on the internet nowadays offering the possibility to select support for individual monks, nuns and projects. Colourful photos tell the stories of a child, a monk or nun and an interested sponsor may pick his or her choice through the websites of various organisations.[29]

In 2007 this virtual reciprocity caters for the needs of the greater part of the Dolanji community and replaces most of the system of mutual care as it was common in Tibet and Nepal. While this system was rooted in a religiously inspired reciprocity – religious actions to make safe the good for both the individual and the community – the foundation of the virtual reciprocity lies mostly in charity, with preference for specific groups such as women and children. Western sponsors prefer to support the development of activities that further good education and improve prospects for women inside the religious system. In doing so the sponsors, wittingly or unwittingly, influence the way the religious community is run. Sponsors donate money for a certain project, and want to see that specific project succeed. The way the money is spent must be specified precisely. In this way interaction is set into motion between Western preferences and a traditional Tibetan monastic system. Western sponsors actively contribute to redefining the role and position of a nun.

The time and energy needed to repair the road that was washed away in the rain season caused a lot of concern. Certainly access to the convent is a problem and it is hard to keep supplies coming, but the administration was also worried about the possible delay of the construction of the dormitories and workshops. These activities are paid for with funds raised by an American organisation. Shortly before His Holiness left for America, a video film was made to show that the work advances according plan. I was repeatedly asked to make as many photos as possible of the repair activities and the work on the buildings, with the intention to show them to the sponsors in America.

It is worthwhile to realise that by far the most organisations raising funds for the Bon in America are led by women. This partly explains the preference of the organisations for themes and projects benefiting women.

---

28   Interview, Geshe Shenphen Samdup, 20 August 2007.
29   http://www.bonfoundation.org/cc_menrichild.html

4.1.2 Gender, the Body and the Religious Praxis

During my fieldwork the nuns focused their studies on two important religious customs: 1) the Chamma praxis, which is an element of the sutra and is linked with the heart mantra's, and 2) the Chod praxis, part of the tantric tradition which centres around the notion that one must learn to disconnect oneself from all possible concepts, the personal body included. In principle both men ands women may study these teachings.

According to the Buddhist tradition the Chod praxis was first introduced in Tibet by a woman, Yogini Machig Labdron, and is usually practiced by women (Allione 2000, 165-205). The Bon tradition claims that (elements of) the Chod customs were in use before Buddhism was introduced in Tibet, and therefore are part of the ritual Bon praxis. (Norbu N 1995, 102).

Figure 4.1 Icon of Chamma

Both ritual traditions focus on woman-hood. The Chod praxis was introduced by a woman and Chamma is the outstanding example of the female principle: the mother. She is seen as the loving mother of wisdom.

The nuns and monks I have interviewed do not mention typical female customs, though they refer to differences in the nature of men and women as the origin of the different kinds of praxis. In almost all interviews the biological differences between the sexes are said to be the reason for the differences in contemplation and the reason that women do not take the same vows as men. Men follow the curriculum for the ritual praxis, but may also choose to follow training for the Geshe degree. For women, on the other hand, practising a ritual path such as Chod or a retreat is considered the better way. Usually it is added that though Tonpa Sherab did not distinguish between men and women, differences in nature have created this divergence. It is also said that the reasons for disparity are culturally embedded. According to this perspective men follow a cognitive path, while the way of women is in the first place tied up with emotion.

The Lopan* has the following explanation:

"Tonpa Sherab has never said anything to explain why women should take more vows than men. But in my view of the teaching of the Bon, women are more sensitive than men. That means that for women praxis is easier then for men. The feelings of men are stronger, stronger in the meaning of wavering in their faith. It is more difficult for them to connect with the praxis."

> "We call that Nydung, which means that it explains the way in which men and women learn things in a different manner. In fact we say that male feelings, the emotions, are stronger; the anger and the evil just are. Feminine feelings, emotions, have to do more with connecting themselves with something. Tonpa Sherab offered his teachings to both men and women, quite different from Buddhism. The mother of the Buddha stood up and asked if he was willing to include women in his teachings. That is the history of Buddhism. That doesn't exist in the Bon tradition: on from the beginning there is word about men and women who may take the vows. And we do notice how these differences have developed in their own way. It is true that the monasteries for men outnumber the monasteries for women. I suppose that it has to do with the social and cultural history of Tibet and the region of the Himalayas. Most women were cut of from education. The village where I grew up, for instance, numbered many women practising faith, but they had not learned to read or write. They learned everything they needed by keeping it in their hearts, the oral tradition. Most women work very hard, in their home. Education was never open to them. Another reason is that the public and social domain was and is male territory. And there is the domain of politics, of course. The idea never was to put women on a lower scale, or in a lower position. It is, it feels like a natural cultural development. My feeling is that Tonpa Sherab never distinguished between men and women, and when I go over our history I cannot find differences between men and women. He treated everyone equally. The differences are revealed in society. But many Bonpo texts mention women who have reached enlightenment. It is possible for women to reach enlightenment. I

have told about the Nydung, which is connected with suffering, with samsara. A woman may suffer, but will try to relieve the suffering sooner than a man would. For women it is easier to start practising." [30]

The Lopan expresses what many of the men I have spoken with, tried to say: differences between men and women are not religiously inspired, but stem from social, cultural and economic customs in Tibet and the Tibetan upland plains.

The Lopan also refers to something else. That is that men are used to shape their life, whether in a group or in a monastery, in a religious way and that they can choose from a multitude of good examples. For women there are far less religious role models available. The female role models found in Bon history mainly refer to women who have grown individually to an exceptional high spiritual level. They did not come to enlightenment by being a nun in a convent, but they reached the highest state while living outside the walls of a monastery. My fieldwork clearly shows that most nuns living in Redna Menling do not have any monasterial background references and that monasterial life didn't play an important role in their daily life. This in contrast with the spiritual life they experience inside their home. Lopan makes this very clear:

"You have met Rinchen Sangmo, she is called Ani Gampo. Her mother is a Nagma, a Nagma from my lineage. Nagma means that long ago she was initiated in tantric praxis, that she took the tantric vows. Rinchen Sangmo's father is a Nagpa. There are special ceremonies carried out by men and women together, unlike the ceremonies in a monastery. The men and women come together and they also work together. They pray, they chant*, build, eat and drink together. Together they look after the monastery, not in the way of collecting money. They maintain the monastery, donating their own money. There are special retreats for Nagmas and Nagpas. The training takes three years. I did that when I was young. It takes three years, as I said, and there is plenty of time fore praxis, for ceremonies for the special gods and goddesses, for praying and chanting every morning, reciting mantras and doing prostrations. And after three years you are a Nagma or a Nagpa. My mother was a Nagma too, or as it is also called: jomo. But it is a tradition that is in danger of disappearing. In my village everything is falling into decay. The jomo monastery we had is in ruin now, and especially the jomo temple has been devastated. The reason is that in modern society such a system cannot be kept alive. People send their children to school, and after finishing school they no longer want to return to the old system. They no longer want to be active in the old tantric system. They move to the cities to find a living. Others go into business and try to make money that way. That used to be impossible, but these days being a businessman has become so much easier. There is much more contact between different regions. That is the reason an old tradition, a practising tradition, is about to disappear. Five years ago I went back to the village where I was born. No one was in retreat there; hardly anyone was using the monastery. This year they have sent seven children here, to this monastery. I have made contact with older people in the region where I was born and asked them to do their religious praxis in the monastery, in any case in wintertime. There is no work in winter and I can

---

30   Interview, Menri Lopon Rinpoche, 14 October 2007.

support them financially. So far they have not said they will. They are very busy and after the winter they will go to Kathmandu. Then there is nothing that I can do anymore. It means losing a tradition that gives women a prominent position in our religion. Modern times also bring about loss of oral tradition, and that also means that female lines of descend are about to disappear." [31]

In an exchange with Lama Khemsar Rinpoche I said that I had the impression that women gifted with leadership are hardly visible inside the Bon. He reacted promptly:

"What do you mean by invisible? Many women are very wise, but it is a wisdom not found in books. These women learn everything by storing their knowledge in their heart, before passing it on, from mother to daughter. It is the oral tradition. You will only hear these stories when you sit down and talk with these women." [32]

What the inhabitants of Redna Menling monastery tell about religious life in their native villages, how it is and was experienced, corresponds with the descriptions given by the Lopan and Lama Khemsar. But when the nuns mention the differences in religious practice between men and women, they do not describe the differences they saw or experienced at home. Most of all they tell they have to take different vows, being a nun. They explain the differences from gender and from the consequences of celibacy. Some of the nuns think that women are more vulnerable than men and should be more careful. This vulnerability is interpreted as having more responsibility, because for a woman a mistake may have more consequences than for a man: she may get pregnant.

Tsundu, age 23, sees it this way:

"There isn't really any difference between monks and nuns. We all learn the same things. The only difference is that if nuns do something bad, they may get children. Monks don't. The nuns are often blamed for the bad things. For instance, when monks and nuns have sex, the nuns get the blame." [33]

Nuns have to meet a high moral standard, where rules and regulations about the physical body are concerned. In the story of Monlam that is illustrated sharply:

"There were many nuns in the valley close to our village, in our village itself there were none. Some girls from my valley went there to become a nun. Most of us couldn't go there, our families wouldn't let us. It wasn't a Bon monastery, but it was also not a very serious monastery. The people in my village were ashamed of such a monastery. A group of the nuns from this monastery went on pilgrimage to Bodh Gayha and there they met with boys from Nepal and Bhutan. Some of them became pregnant. The people in my village saw that and said that these nuns were not serious nuns." [34]

---

31 Interview, Menri Lopon Rinpoche, 14 October 2007.
32 Fieldnotes, Conversation with Lama Khemsar Rinpoche, 23 August 2007.
33 Interview, Ani Tsundu Sangmo, 4 September 2007.
34 Interview, Ani Monlam Wangmo, 6 September 2007.

The monks with whom I discussed the differences between men and women, between monks and nuns, pointed mainly what they call emotional and/or mental differences.

Geshe Nyima Dakpa said it this way:

> *"It is commonly known that women take more vows than men. It has to do with the rules laid down in the Vinaya. According to me, these rules go back to the differences between men and women, both mentally and physically. I think that women have to cope with other inner processes than men, and these differences express themselves in a different way of studying. I don't think it has to do with potential. I think men and women can reach the same level, be it in a different way, following a different path."* [35]

His Holiness underlined the connection between samsara, the existence on all levels including the world we live in now, and the differences between men and women. According to His Holiness differences between the sexes did not play a role in the time the Bon was founded. Neither has the sex of a person any bearing on the ultimate goal, reaching Nirvana. Enlightenment, which in the end is the goal of all religious deeds and actions, doesn't depend on gender. An enlightened person may assume a male or a female form, but the spirit is not male or female. Being born in the body of a man or a woman, with its limitations and possibilities, is a matter of karma, is determined by what a person still has to learn from life.[36]

As far as gender is concerned in Buddhist philosophy, these views partly coincide with the conclusions Rita Gross laid down in *Buddhism after Patriarchy* (Gross 2003, 115-116).

- Every important phase in the development of Buddhism includes viewpoints about women, varying from straightforward women-unfriendly to idea's compassionate towards womanhood: being a woman is a harsh and hard fate in the 'cycle of life'. Both notions are found in the texts available for research, usually apart from each other.

- The many philosophical discussions held inside Buddhism have given rise to several schools. In these schools the position of women is not left untouched. Certain groups articulate very discriminating views about womanhood and the role of women. Others, however, maintain the principle that the dharma as such is neither male nor female. Eventually it was Tibetan Buddhism that developed a system incorporating the female principle in the endeavour to come to enlightenment in the end.

- Every school inside Buddhism holds negative ideas about women, but all considered there is not such a thing as gender in the practising of the dharma.

---

35 Interview, Geshe Nyima Dakpa, 12 August 2007.
36 Interview, His Holiness Lungtok Tenpai Nyima, 1 September 2007.

Gross also notices that in Tibet and in regions under Tibetan influence women have more opportunity for a religious career than in India, even though men wield religious power. She concludes that Tibetan Buddhism offers women more freedom to pursue a religious life outside the family. Which doesn't mean that in Tibet all religious options are open to women.

In Gross' view the female monastic tradition has not grown to the prestige and power owned by the male monastic tradition, partly due to the absence of a tradition which allows women a full ordination. In spite of a system developed in Tibetan Buddhism which allowed women to hold a prestigious position by becoming a Yogini, women do not occupy a prominent place in Tibetan history (Gross 2003, 83-88).

The situation inside the Bon isn't substantially different. Nuns certainly lack the possibilities monks have in the religious praxis and the monastic tradition doesn't offer women the prestige it holds for men. Yet the opportunities seem more promising than the Buddhist practice, because of the theoretical possibility for women to receive a full ordination and because of the system of Nagpa and Nagma that offers them a position in the religious system through the oral tradition.

The stories of the nuns of Redna Menling make clear, however, that they do not aspire the religious position of the Nagma. The margins the monks enjoy are the yardstick to measure the possibilities and impossibilities they experience in being a nun. The nuns feel that within these margins the physical differences between the sexes and the values and standards applied to physicality in dealing with monks and nuns is given extra weight.

4.1.3 Theoretical Intermezzo: Gender and the Physical Body

In essence the goal of all initial religious praxis is control of the physical body, speech and mind: controlling the breath, controlling what we say and controlling the mental images. This is seen as the gateway towards a state of contemplation.

The nuns of Redna Menling measure the differences between men and women (monks and nuns) in physical differences, not in differences referring to the ritual praxis or to learning the praxis. That could be due to the stage the nuns of Redna Menling are in, at present. The nuns are only beginning to familiarise with the praxis and cannot muster the support of a monastic tradition of their own. So far the emphasis is on learning to read and write Tibetan. Where physicality is discussed, the nuns contribute in terms of celibacy.

When there are questions about the effect of the body on a nun's praxis, most women can't find an answer, or say: *"The body is the body."* And if there is an answer, it is about the bodily sensation for instance when singing mantras or sitting at prayer services in the temple (goose bumps, stiff, cold).

As is apparent from the previous paragraph, physicality and gender questions are translated into sexual differences and the consequences of sexual contact for nuns. The monks do not express physical differences in terms of sexuality, but in terms of explaining why the praxis of women in general differs from the praxis of men.

In her book *Natural Symbols* Mary Douglas finds a link between religion, its expression in rituals and the way society organises itself. The ritual or the rituals are a means of communication. A ritual is an expression reproducing and mirroring social relations. According to Douglas the body and the way the body is treated in the praxis first and foremost telltales the way a society is shaped in social structures, including hierarchy and social roles. She developed two ideas to work this out: *group* and *grid*.

Group stands for the rules society (or an organisation) enforces upon the individual. The individual will adapt to the pressure applied by the group. When it comes to structured role patterns, a monastery is a perfect tool. Douglas has found that a person living in such a structure will try to bring the system of social demands in line with his or her personal perception. How much control a group, or a society, has over or on a body in general should be seen as a degree of the amount of social control.

Grid is the name Douglas attaches to the freedom the individual has to adjust to or to escape from the social pressure of the group. *Grid* refers to an individual obligation towards the group felt by a group member and to what it takes to maintain oneself in the group. *Grid* should be seen as a structure, a classification, as a symbolic system (Douglas, 1996, 78)

Douglas expects a person to try to balance the system of group pressure with the level he or she experiences. She looks at the body as the perfect tool to express the feelings symbolising the system in which the individual person moves about. The amount of control exerted by a society and a system is mirrored in the way control is exerted over the body.

Douglas writes:

> *"Consequently I now advance the hypotheses that bodily control is an expression of social control – abandonment of bodily control in ritual responds to the requirements of a social experience which is being expressed. Furthermore, there is little prospect of successful imposing bodily control without the correspondent social forms. And lastly, the same drive that seeks harmoniously to relate the experience of physical and social must affect ideology. Consequently, when once the correspondence between bodily and social controls is traced, the basis will be laid for considering co-varying attitudes in political thought and in theology" (Douglas 1996, 78).*

In Chapter 3 the stories the women tell illustrate how they try to reconcile the circumstances they cope with, with the situation they live in, monasterial life. Their expectations of life to come is expressed conform the rules and standards of monasterial life. This is the expression of an individual psychological process of adaptation. However, that individual process encompasses the collective process, stimulating the individuals, each with her own background, to present themselves as a group (monasterial community) and able to develop a normative *communitas*.

Control of the body, safeguarding celibacy, has an important place in the monasterial community. Control over the body and over various bodily functions is an important aspect of ritual praxis. Celibacy is one of the most important vows a nun takes. It means to renounce gender-associated roles such as spouse and mother.

The distance towards the body in daily life in Dolanji is seen most poignantly in the geographical distance created consciously between the monasteries for men and for women. The village and the river form a natural fence, a barrier between nuns and monks, or, in the words of His Holiness: *"The aim is to ensure that there are witnesses of the contacts between monks and nuns."*[37] In other words, it takes witnesses to make sure that things that are not allowed do not come to pass, meaning breaking the rule of celibacy.

The monastery of men on the one bank of the river, on the other bank the monastery for women and the village containing the lay community of Dolanji stands in between. The nuns greatly respect this natural barrier and when crossing the barrier they change the way they behave. A good example is the visit I paid to the Menri Monastery in the company of three nuns. From afar the nuns spotted the abbot and his escort. I myself was still unaware of him, but the three nuns started to check their attire and clothing right away, making sure they wouldn't give offence in any way.

One day some nuns came to visit the guesthouse where I stayed. After sitting and talking on the balcony of my room we went to the refectory to have some tea. Instantly the attire of the nuns changed: they bow to greet the monks present, even though they hold the same rank, and they start to serve tea. The monks accepted this service as a matter of fact and did not return the respectful bowing of the nuns.

The nuns may take part in rituals in the Menri Monastery, such as processions around the temple. But when they do, special rules come into effect regarding place and rank. The rule is that the monks walk in front, regardless of age and seniority. The nuns follow at the end of the procession, behind the youngest monk, even if he is only three years old.

Within the confines of their own monastery there are other habits. The strict clothing rules are often partly ignored and in a casual way there is bodily contact. All these phenomena disappear instantly, when monks enter the grounds of the convent. The nuns realise sharply that even on their own territory they should take care not to give offence. So they adjust their clothing and adapt their body language to the prevailing circumstances.

The monks also respect the geographical barrier, but have less embarrassment stepping over it. One reason is that the monks are responsible for supplying the convent. But it are also monks who do the teaching, as well as the coordination and control of the ongoing building activities. It would seem that for the monks the convent is much more a part of their domain than the other way round. *'The other side'*, the women say when talking about the monastery for men

---

37 Interview, His Holiness Lungtok Tenpai Nyima, 1 September 2007.

These differences also come to light in the religious praxis. Nuns lack the respect that monks enjoy, being regarded as religious specialists. From this respect the monks derive an extra degree of freedom. Keeping the other sex at a safe distance is a characteristic aspect of celibacy. When the delicate balance between monks and nuns is disturbed because monks are deemed to have more knowledge, nuns revert to physical distance to show they are good nuns.

During fieldwork I have witnessed how monks entered the temple of the women without hesitation. Yet no nun will even consider entering the temple of the men. The same can be said of other buildings, such as the kitchen and the storage rooms. It is a way of underlining status and position.

Controlling physicality in terms of controlling sexuality and not giving offence seems to be the way for nuns to prove that they are 'good nuns'.

4.1.4 The Impact of the Research

Conversations and interviews with the nuns of Redna Menling form the basis of the chapters 3 and 4. These stories offer us a glimpse in the world of someone else. The fact that I had come to sit down and listen to what the nuns were to tell me certainly had its impact on this religious community. All at once the nuns were a topic. At whiles I had to take care to find the right heading between my interpretation of the stories and the context in which I should be hearing them. Sometimes a considerable gap looms between this context, as the nuns experience it, and the views of a layperson or those in charge of the convent.

Problems concerning the curriculum, the absence of a daily management and the position of the girls who did not choose to enter the convent were put on the agenda and entered the discussions. Time and again I was asked to write down my findings, in order to further a greater variety of lessons and to promote the chance of a full ordainment.

Really complicated is the position of the nuns who entered the convent involuntarily. An alternative solution is not available, the choice is between staying and going back. The monastery, the religious community, lives up to its social obligations in sheltering the girls. My personal view is that often it is hard to digest that young girls more or less against their will are confined in a monastery. On return to their parents, the girls risk an insecure future. Neither Nepal nor India offers possibilities for schooling of girls of their age and level of education.

Most nuns find it interesting to tell me their story, but at the same time they do not feel their story is something special. In the beginning it was hard to find a balance between openness and socially acceptable answers, but in due time confidence and openness increased. In the first place because I did not only want to talk and listen to them, but I also lent a hand (as with rebuilding the road), accepted their food, relaxed on their beds, followed their classes, joined them in their temple and conformed to their rules as much as I could.

Telling me their story sometimes changed the outlook of the girls on their own position. They felt taken serious and as such started to take a serious look at their own situation, role and possibilities. The mere fact that they could speak out their hope that at some time in the future there would be Geshe training available to them was a major step. It made the nuns of Redna Menling give words to their dreams and expectations, with a central role for themes like studying and becoming a learned person.

Chapter 5

Conclusion | The Nuns of Redna Menling

5.1 Introduction

In this final chapter I present a concise outline of place and position of the nuns of Redna Menling in the religious tradition of the Bon, in order to meet the goal of research, as specified in chapter 1.

The results of my fieldwork, in which interviews and (participating) observation are given a central role, I have complemented with a study of available relevant literature. In this way I found a way to picture the position of a nun on different levels, and sketch in particular the mutual influences of the levels involved. From the micro level - the individual nuns – I have looked at the relationship at the meso level – the monastery, the concrete monasterial tradition – and the macro level – the Bon religion and its history.

I started chapter 1 at the macro level. This is a complex history, as Bon and Buddhism turn out to be related in a certain way, where organisation and systems of belief are concerned. But history also shows that the Bon has succeeded in holding its ground as an independent religion, with a prominent place for its origins, attributing an equal position to women. The belief that Tonpa Sherap, the mythical founder of the Bon, treated men and women equally seems to be denied by the fact that nuns are virtually invisible in the present day Bon tradition in exile.

Chapter 2 specifically follows developments in the exiled Bon, its community in Dolanji-India, the context the nuns of Redna Menling live and in which the present day monastic tradition is shaped.

After evaluation of this context the nuns of Redna Menling come to speak for themselves in the chapters 3 and 4. These narratives make up the content of the main source of the thesis, in which I have tried to find an answer on the research questions.

The research among the nuns of Redna Menling at first offers an insight in the position of nuns in the Bon religion. The scholarly work covered new ground, as I did not succeed in finding actual research into the female monastic Bon tradition. The available research, though done in Tibet, and focuses on place, position and motivation of women entering monasteries, is limited to Buddhist nuns and nunneries. These studies should be interpreted with care, because followers of the Bon position themselves as members of an independent religion, which should not be linked to Buddhism. I have tried to honour that point of view, bearing in mind that scholarly work exclusively using Buddhist sources will produce a distorted picture of the Bon. That is why I have chosen for fieldwork with interviews and participating local observations as most important instruments. I want to use the stories of the nuns of Redna Menling as a starting point. By enriching these narratives with information gathered in interviews and meetings with informers from the wider community, with fieldwork observations and with theoretical surveys, I succeeded in uplifting this micro level study to new insights in the position of nuns in a community in exile (the meso level) and in the Bon religion as a whole (macro level). The interlocking effects of these separate levels and its significance for the role and position of the nuns I will clarify in the next paragraph, along with the effects on important questions such as gender relations, celibacy and ritual praxis.

5.2 Macro Level: The Nuns Place inside the Bon

Traces of a monastic tradition for women inside the Bon are very hard to find. In the interviews the nuns, all native from the Nepalese highlands, acknowledge that prior to entering the convent they hardly had any dealings with a female monastic tradition. Rita Gross underlines that though Tibetan Buddhism allows women to fulfil religious positions, the authority over religious institutions has always been in the hand of men (Gross 1993). The Bon religion gives a similar picture. The monastic tradition of the Bon takes shape in the 11th century, following the example of Buddhism that at the time is finding a foothold in Tibet and the Tibetan uplands (Kvaerne 1995). The monasteries founded then were open to men only.

The historic picture emerging from the views of His Holiness, the Lopan and the Geshes is no different. Even in the past the Bon religion in Tibet and Nepal did not make space for a female monastic tradition, comparable to the monasteries for men. Stark is the contrast to the explicit message of Tonpa Sherab, the founder of the Bon that his teachings were meant for men and women alike. That is why men and women are supposed to have similar chances for development. It is also one of the main reasons to allow women a place in the present monastic system.

In *An Historical Overview of the Bon Religion* Samten Karmay concludes that scholarly research so far has focussed on the (male) monastic tradition (Karmay 2001, 55-81). This tradition meets the eye especially in Tibet, but also covers an important sector of the Bon tradition, where religion is perceived and shaped through religious responsibilities linked to lineage and flourishes in the shelter of the family. The position women occupy in this tradition is impressive and both the Nagma and the Nagpa have their own responsibilities in the religious tasks and functions they fulfil in village life and in the relations they keep with the local monasteries. The lines of ancestry make sure the tasks and functions are transferred to both men and women.

The way these religious tasks, as painted by the nuns and other spokespersons, are perceived and accomplished is in keeping with Geoffrey Samuels' analyses in *Civilised Shamans*. He distinguishes between Clerical Buddhism, characterised by a vivid monasterial tradition supported by written texts, and Shamanic or Tantric Buddhism developed from the oral tradition (Samuel 1993).

At this level the history of the origin of the Bon seems to be more in line with the professed equality of men and women. Women are present and fulfil a significant role, and as Lama Khemsar Rinpoche said: "These women form a significant part of the Bon religion, but to find out one needs to sit down and talk with them. They are part of the oral tradition and do not appear in books and writings." [38]

The meetings with the Lopan made clear that this tradition is in danger in the Nepalese uplands. The region is laid open more and more, economic change takes place and opportunities for trade multiply. More and more people decide to move to the towns and cities, temporarily or for longer periods, threatening the vitality of old traditions.

Even the monasteries, for centuries the centres upholding this tradition, find it hard to keep up maintenance and are in danger of disappearing. These parallel developments threaten the survival of a tradition offering women a possibility to be religiously active and to fulfil a widely recognised religious position. As a result women have to look around for new opportunities. This gives monasterial life a more prominent position, also for women.

5.3 Meso Level: Reasons to Profess and Life in a Monastic Community

Though the Menri Monastery was founded especially as a place for Tibetan exiles, none of the nuns of Redna Menling is a Tibetan refugee. The nuns were all born in Nepal. In fact nuns were rarely seen among the exiles in the first years after Tibet was occupied. For women or nuns it was difficult to leave the country, and the journey across the mountains to India is physically demanding and dangerous. Many nuns were forced to revoke their vows and start a secular life (Tsomo 2003, 346-347). Information I was able to collect during my visit to Tibet (2006) and during my fieldwork in Dolanji (2007), indicates that since some years monasteries may be rebuild in Tibet. Although restrictions are imposed, men and women can anew take up life in the monasteries. That may be one of the reasons that so few women seek refuge in the nunnery in Dolanji.

Karma Lekse Tsomo stipulates in *Tibetan Nuns: New Roles and Possibilities* that the convents founded in exile are deemed very attractive, most of all because of their improved educational programs. By far the most of the nuns who entered Buddhist monasteries in India, were born in exile (Tsomo 2003, 346-347)

The statements of the nuns of Redna Menling make clear that, similar to developments among Buddhist nuns, the educational opportunities offered are considered extremely attractive. All nuns interviewed indicate that the possibility to study is one of the main reasons to enter the convent. Born and bred in Nepal, these women had little chance of going to school, due to the circumstances at home and the economic and geographical situation.

---

38 Fieldnotes, Conversation with Lama Khemsar Rinpoche, 23 August 2007.

Studying, combined with taking religious vows, seems to constitute a plausible combination in the tradition these women grew up in. To study, and to have graduated, increases someone's status in the community and adds to the likelihood of a successful reincarnation for the whole of the family.

Though the women and girls have varied reasons to enter the monastery, they have in common this opportunity to accomplish their studies. The relatively large number of girls living in care of the convent without taking the vows, adds to this image.

And because the education in Redna Menling is free of charge, the influx is unlikely to decrease, even if the situation in Nepal gets better.

The women each have chosen to enter Redna Menling individually and together they form the first female Bon community in exile.

The motives to profess could be split up in three main categories:
1. Practical considerations, such a the possibility to study
2. Religiously inspired
3. Political and economical circumstances in the Nepalese uplands

Most of all the practical considerations (possibilities to study) and the political circumstances have led to an increase in the number of women seeking refuge in Redna Menling.

Yet I doubt that it is the only reason for expansion of the monasterial community in exile. A number of developments coincided in a few years. As early as 2004 there was a small group of women seeking ways to fulfil their religious tasks as nuns. However, they lacked a place of their own, a convent. The presence of these women in the community acted as a catalyst, making the male religious community aware of women longing to be nuns and fulfilling religious tasks in a monastic tradition.

Prominent members of the religious community of Dolanji recognised the signs of time and dedicated themselves to enable women to become full members of the monastic tradition.

This change coincides with a growing interest in the West for women inside the monastic tradition of the Bon. It turns out that sufficient financial means are available to provide good facilities for the nuns of Dolanji. Fundraising in behalf of the monastery brings to light that globalisation is a major influence here.

Fundraising also takes over from the tradition of religiously based reciprocity. The fact that women, in spite of tradition do not have to cater for their own upkeep (clothes and food), attracts young women from in particular poor families. Some women, who do not have a Bon family background, nevertheless choose the Redna Menling convent to profess.

The variety of motives among the women, the lack of experience of monasterial life, the low level of education have led to the creation of a community that is not yet ready to fully live the religious practice.

On the other hand, studying and partly doing the religious practise together forms the heart of the community of nuns. It has been the impetus to the formation of a normative *communitas* (Turner, 1969, 132). Characteristic for that community is the presence of a liminality, a transitional situation. Within the confines of this liminality a social structure develops, adopting the characteristics of a permanent social structure. The outside world sees and treats Redna Menling as a monasterial community, regardless the motives of the individual women. The values and standards applied inside the religious community refer to how a 'good' nun should behave and which obligations and consequences come from living in a monastery.

5.4 Gender, Celibacy and Ritual Praxis

The liminality caused by entering a convent can be interpreted in several ways. In my view the liminality of the Redna Menling community at this moment is set by the fact that all members are both student and women.

The eventual aim of a woman professing, is to become a nun. But a path of learning, leading to control over the complex religious praxis, separates the moment of professing and the actual attainment of the status of nun. Moreover, several vows have to be taken. Until all are taken, the woman remains a novice, and as such she will remain in the state of liminality. Being students is the main factor determining the relation between the convent (the nuns) and the male monastery (the monks). But in general it is unlikely that the ordination of a group of nuns would eliminate the evident differences between monks and nuns.

The fact that they are women, who have to do without the support of a thriving monastic female tradition, will lead to a lasting leading position for men in the religious community, in spite of an eventual dissolving of the differences in education. The views of the Geshes in particular, underline how gender is the decisive element in the possibilities open to women. Most remarkable is the conviction that due to their nature the path for women to reach enlightenment is different from the path for men.

Not one of the nuns mentioned a female nature leading them on a separate path towards enlightenment. So far the women define the differences between them and the monks in terms of education, and in the second place in terms of the possible consequences of breaking celibacy. They experience celibacy as the essence of the vows they take when entering the monastery. That view gives physicality and the standards and values attached to it in the religious community, a regulatory influence. Distance and proximity, in which body and bodily control are involved, are defined in such phrases. According to the women the most severe implications of celibacy are not having children and not entering a relationship with a man, yet many do not regard married life and raising children a desirable future.

The way women undergo the monasterial community is characterized by the burden of control of bodily functioning. In the interviews the women indicate that when it comes to celibacy nuns are deemed more responsible than the monks involved. They feel that when celibacy is broken, it is the nuns who are held guilty. This puts the heavy load of avoiding any clue that might provoke a breaking of the vows, on the shoulders of the nuns.

This way they aren't only responsible for their own vows, but indirectly also for the vows taken by the men. This is in line with the theory Mary Douglas puts forward in *Natural Symbols*. She comes to the conclusion that the amount of control and structure wielded by a society, is reflected in the way the physical body is brought under control (Douglas, 1996).

A recurring theme in the meetings with prominent leaders of the Menri Monastery, but also with key persons in the lay community, is the idea that the way nuns and monks practise their lives should remain pure. Starting point is control of desire, hatred and ignorance. The emphasis is on individual spiritual development and on obedience to the monastic authority.

The increasing pressure of outside influences threatens these principles; monks travel around the world, television is present all the time, nuns watch Harry Potter and Hindu love stories and Westerns sponsors pour out their views on man/woman relations.

Both the religious and lay community exercise control over these areas, and both are trying to come to terms with the gap between outside influences and their own principles. The wish to remain pure and true to the doctrine is evident, but it is impossible to stay free of the influences of a globalising world.

Physicality and controlling of the body through celibacy, is a recurring theme in the life of the women of Redna Menling. In particular the question of how to behave towards men. For monks that subject plays a minor role.

In many respects the nuns depend on the men of the monastery and it is this dependency that creates a sharp awareness of what is allowed and what is not. The control over the body (refrain from sexual activities and obnoxious behaviour) proves that a woman is a good nun or novice.

For the religious community of Dolanji the convent is a new phenomenon, attracting a lot of attention, inside and outside the community. As a result there is an increasing pressure on the nuns of Redna Menling to adhere strictly to written and unwritten rules.

My argument is that the nucleus of the community of nuns is the ritual praxis. A ritual praxis that cannot yet be lived to the full extend, because the nuns are not yet fully ordained, and a comprehensive educational program is still absent. Such a program could further women to present themselves as ritual experts. That would allow women access to a more fully fledged role inside and outside the Dolanji community. The communities of men and of women both see speeding up the development of an educational program as a major step towards achieving the full potential of the Redna Menling monastery.

The ritual praxis consists of two main components. First of all, the praxis should lead towards an individual path in the direction of a superior incarnation and in the end, enlightenment. The other component is rendering service to the community by carrying out rituals, and in which the reciprocity between lays and the religious community is essential. As it is common to pay for rituals, this reciprocal effect could boost the economic independence of the Redna Menling monastery.

It is up to the individual practising, be it man or woman, how to actually fill in the ritual praxis. There are several possibilities, as I have shown in Chapter 1: following a Geshe-training, living in a monastery with close ties with the surrounding communities, or doing practise in so-called hermitages. Every day life shows that in Dolanji the women do not yet have this choice.

Economic independence of the Redna Menling monastery is also to be found outside the confines of the ritual praxis. Some nuns receive training to become a Thangka painter. Painting and producing thangka's could become a source of income.

The greatest whish of the nuns is to have their own Geshe training program. Judging from the present level of education of the nuns it may seem a distant wish, but that situation could change for the girls now in care of the convent, visiting the secular school in the village. The nuns are convinced that proper educational training to be a ritual expert opens the door to a promising future and offers a position more equal to the monks.

The opposition between the principle that men and women are equal - referring to the origin of the Bon - and daily reality lacking a tradition rooted in a flourishing female monasterial tradition, is experienced most poignantly is the absence of a fully operational ritual praxis. This has shifted the emphasis towards celibacy and differences in carrying out the ritual praxis.

5.5 Epilogue

Samten G. Karmay describes Buddhism and Bon as the two faces of the same coin. I have found, however, that the absence of research into the place and position of nuns inside the Bon makes it very hard to get a clear view of that side of the coin. The fieldwork in Dolanji has been the first step in bringing detailed vision.

Books and articles may be read, mental processes will take place and evolve towards ideas that are projected upon the field to be researched. The effect may be that only one side of the coin is worked out. This is what initially influenced my views and may have led to a surprise later on. In the course of my fieldwork I soon had to acknowledge that there were no women of Tibetan descend among the nuns of Redna Menling. This was something I had not anticipated from the theoretical orientation of available literature. I found out that the area covered by the Bon extends well outside Tibet. I fully trusted the way the Dolanji community presents itself, as an outstanding example of Tibetan exiles, as is common among exiled communities.

The impact of globalising factors, like the way fundraising and financial support from Europe and America have evolved, should be taken into account when forming an idea of these communities. The Dolanji community is far more complex than I ever anticipated when setting up my fieldwork.

Still many questions remain unanswered. The stories of the nuns of Redna Menling and their place and position inside the exiled Bon community have turned out to be just a first step. Multidisciplinary research is needed to really find and interpret the place of a female monastic tradition in the history of the

Bon. More research is also needed into the oral tradition, in which women seem to occupy a significant position.

The following questions might find a place in the extended research project: Is there a change for women detectable inside the Bon, where a shift from the oral tradition towards a monastic tradition is concerned? Which developments await Redna Menling, in the years to come? What means and efforts are going to be invested into the educational program the women themselves wanted so dearly? Does the setting up of a dedicated curriculum, once realised, holds the promise to attract Bon-women and nuns from Tibet and Nepal to the Redna Menling convent? A wide scope of research subjects is waiting.

By presenting my project the nuns were turned into a subject of daily conversation. That mere fact has made the project worthwhile. People have become aware that though tradition states that men and women, or monks and nuns, are equal, daily practice may prove otherwise.

'Your nuns', the nuns of Redna Menling were referred to in conversations about my project with all kinds of people. 'My nuns', who came to see me as the ambassador of their wishes and interests.

As a result the nuns in general and the nuns of Redna Menling in particular have become a subject of importance. I sincerely hope that this research project will be a first step leading to a full mapping of nuns and women inside the Bon. For that they can be found, is evident now.

To end with, the hospitality and openness with which the community has welcomed me is of everlasting value. Every question was answered, every wish was accommodated to if possible, I was forgiven whatever mistakes I made in the daily protocol of the monastic community. The lasting impression all of this has made on me, is a major reason that this research project was transformed in so much more than just a project.

Appendix 1

Glossary

Ani Title for a nun in Tibet and in areas where Tibetan Buddhism and Bon are practised. Ani la, is a respectful title.

Bodhisattva A being that has reached enlightenment.

Bonpo Follower of the Bon.

Chamma 'The loving mother'. Main goddess in the Bon, also called Yum Chen Sherab Chamma, 'the great loving mother of wisdom'.

Chanting The reciting of sacred texts.

Chod A ritual praxis within the tantric system. The focus is on learning to detach the conditioned self. Especially letting go of the fear of death and dying to play a central role. In the Chod praxis a bell and a damaru (hand drum) are used.

Geshe Title of a monk after he has completed his training in the scholarly tradition of the Bon.

Hermitage A hermits cabin or an area with several cabins where monks or nuns can retire.

Kanjur 'The translation of the word', forms together with the Tenjur the main text in the Bon. It contains the teachings of the Sutra, Tantra and higher meditations. Within the Bon it is also known as 'the nine ways of Bon': the five paths of the fruit and the four paths of the cause.

Karma (karmic) Literally 'seed'. All acts and thoughts have consequences both in this life now and in future lives.

Kor-Ra Literally 'circle'. In practice it means to walk around a sacred object, such as a temple, and to lie down regularly on the earth during the walk. The purpose of this religious praxis is the purification of negative karma. It is an act of good merit.

Lama Title for a teacher. Guided by compassion and spirituality the Lama helps and supports other people. A Lama may well be a layperson.

Lopan The head of the dialectical school, the Geshe training. In the absence of the abbot of Menri, the Lopan leads the monastery.

Mantra One sentence, sound or word to be repeated with the aim of learning to focus and control the mind.

Nagma and Nagpa Female and male persons practising religious praxis, often following the tantric tradition.

Oracle Intermediary between men and gods

Prostrations Prostrate oneself on the ground usually at a Kor-Ra, but also as the greeting of a highly respected person.

Reincarnation 'Rebirth', derived from the Latin carne 'again in the flesh'. It represents the belief that the soul is preserved after death and is born again in a new living being.

Rinpoche Literally 'precious', a title for a reincarnate master.

Samsara The chain of rebirths in lives, characterized by suffering. The spiritual practice is aimed to break this chain.

Sang and **Sang ritual** Sang is the traditional Tibetan incense composed of loose herbs. In the Sang ritual the surrounding area is purified from negative influences by burning this incense. It also serves to conciliate gods, goddesses and spirits.

Tantra or Tantric tradition The name of the path that is also called the path of rapid enlightenment. A spiritual system in which the balance between the male and the female element plays a major role in the meditation and ritual practices.

Tenjur Forms together with the Kanjur the central text in the Bon. It contains philosophical commentaries and ritual texts.

Thangka or painted scroll. A painted or embroidered banner with pictures of gods, goddesses, important Lama's and historical events. The images serve as an intermediary to which prayers and requests may be addressed. The image is also used as an aid in meditation. In the past a Thangka was also used as an educational tool.

Vinaya Rules and regulations to be observed by monks and nuns. The vows taken are laid down in the Geneyen (8 basic vows), the Tsug Tsang (total 25 vows), the Drang Song vows for monks (total 243) and Gelong vows for nuns (total 360).

Yogini or **Khandroma** 'She who dances in the sky or heaven'. The function of a Yogini or Khandroma is that of a helper or guide. She plays an important role in the tantric tradition as a goddess of wisdom. In this role she is enlightened and appears to others to help them find their way to enlightenment.

Yung Drung Bon 'The Eternal Bon', name of the Bonpo for their religion.

Appendix 2

Letter

Visit to Menri 1982

John Barnett & Vasilka Nicolova

In the summer of 1981 John & I went to California to study with Rosalyn Bruyere – a "laying on of hands" healer, psychic, aura reader and medium. At the end of the 7 weeks it was clear that we needed to return for a longer time.

During these 7 weeks, it was the mediumship that made a profound difference in our lives. The entity that she channelled (the one who spoke through her) was an old Bonpo Master whose last incarnation was 4,000 years ago and whose name was Master Chiang.

At that time Rosalyn had already been channelling Chiang for over 10 years. When he came to her, she went to the library to learn something of Bon. All the books she referred to said it was an ancient Tibetan 'shamanic' religion no 'longer being practiced' or 'now extinct'.

When we returned home to Nova Scotia, John did some research about the Bon religion & discovered that it was not extinct & that there had been a book written by David L. Snellgrove called "The Nine Ways of Bon". David Snellgrove was a professor at the University of London. John wrote him a letter asking about the Bon & how we could get in touch with them. David sent us the name of the Abbot and the address of Menri Monastery in India.

John wrote a letter to the Abbot – S.T. Jongdong – telling him that we would be travelling in his part of the world & asked if it would be appropriate for an American couple to visit his Monastery and that we had learned of the Bon religion from our teacher's spirit guide.

The Abbot's response explained to us how to get there, to bring warm clothing and wanted to know more of our teacher's Bonpo guide – "Is he from the long dead or maybe he is friend from recent dead?" Before we left the USA, we asked Chiang this question & taped his response.

We arrived there at dusk in late November 1982. We had decided to stay for a couple of days but we had to be in Australia in late December -3 ½ weeks went by very quickly at Menri.

We had our meals at the Abbot's residence & had daily conversations with him. The diet consisted of Tea, chapatti, rice & sometimes a green vegetable that was brought for us from a villager's garden. During one of these mealtime conversations we played Chiang's tape. The Abbot asked, "Is your teacher a woman?" – "Yes". He thought for a moment & then said, "There is an ancient Bon prophesy that the Bon would be scattered like the leaves in autumn & would be reunited by a woman."

The Abbot had several questions for us to ask Chiang when we returned.

(There are many stories about our time there that could be added here.)

Upon our return to the USA, we gave a talk & slide show of our trip to Rosalyn's students. Shortly thereafter we move to New Hampshire and continued a correspondence with the Abbot & on occasion sent some support for them.

Rosalyn's community also started sending some support for the children at Menri. In 1989 The Yung Drung Bon Temple Foundation 501c3 non profit organization was formed in California.

Bibliography

Abram, Ido. *Joodse identiteit, over identiteit en imago als beelden en over Joodse identiteit als culturele identiteit.*(Jewish identity, about identy and image as icons and about Jewish identity as a cultural identity) Kampen: Uitgeverij Kok, 1993.

Abram, Ido. *Het raadsel van de Joodse identiteit* (The mystery of Jewish Identity) Amsterdam: Joods Historisch museum, 2006.

Allione, Tsultrim. *Woman of wisdom*, Snow Lion publications. New York: Ithaca, 2000.

Baumer, Christoph. *Bön Die lebendige Ur-religion Tibets.* Graz: ADEVA, 1999.

Bernstorff, Dagmar & Welck, Hubertus von (eds.). *The Tibetan diaspora, exile as challenge.* Delhi: Orient Longman Private Limited, 2003.

Dakpa, Nyima. *Opening the door to Bön.* New York: Snow Lion Publications, 2005.

Douglas, Mary. *Natural Symbols. Explorations in cosmology.* London: Routledge, 1996.

Erikson, Erik H. *Identiteit, jeugd en crisis. De begrippen 'identiteit' en 'identiteitcrisis' in de psychologie en de psychiatrie.* (Identity, youth and crisis. The notion 'identity' and 'crisis of identity' in psychology and psychiatry)Utrecht/Antwerpen: Uitgeverij Het Spectrum, 1971.

Gennep, Arnold van. *The rites of passage. A classic study of cultural celebrations.* Chicago: The University of Chicago press, 1960.

Govinda, Lama Anagarika. *De weg der witte wolken.* (The way of the white clouds) Den Haag: Zuidgroep Bresboek, 1985.

Gross, Rita M. *Buddhism after Patriarchy, a feminist history analyses and reconstruction of Buddhism.* New York: State University of New York press, 1993.

Gyasto, Janet. 'Down with the demons: Reflections on a feminine Ground in Tibet' in Willis, Janice D (ed.). *Feminine Ground: Essays on woman and Tibet.* New York: Snow Lion Publications, 1987, p. 33 – 51.

Havnevik, Hanna. *Tibetan Buddhist nuns.* Oslo: Norwegian University Press, The institute for comparative research in human culture, 1999.

Heldens, Jeanette & Reysoo, Fenneke. 'De kunst van het interviewen: reflecties op het interviewen met een 'guide*(The art of interviewing, reflections on interviewing with a guide) in *Kwalon jaarboek*, 2005.

Hoffmann, Helmut. *Quellen zur Geschichte der tibetischen Bon-Religion.* (Sources of the history of the Tibetan Bon religion) Wiesbaden: Verlag der Akademie der Wissenschaften und der Literatur in Mainz, 1950.

Human Rights Watch. *Children in the Ranks. The Maoists' Use of Child Soldiers in Nepal*, Volume 19, No. 2 (C), Februari 2007.

Karmay, Samten. 'Historical overview of the Bon religion' in Karmay, Samten G. & Watt, Jeff (eds*.). Bon. The magic word, the indigenous religion of Tibet.* New York: Rubin Museum of Art, 2007, p. 55 - 81.

Karmay, Samten G. & Watt, Jeff (eds.). *Bon. The magic word, the indigenous religion of Tibet.* New York: Rubin Museum of Art, 2007.

Kind, Marietta. *Reflektionen zur kulturellen Identität der Tibetischen Bönpo,* (Reflections on the cultural identity of the Tibetan Bonpo) Arbeit vorgelegt zur Tagung der Deutschsprachigen Ethnologinnen und Ethnologen, Wien: 1995.

Kvaerne, Per. 'Aspects of the origin Buddhist tradition in Tibet' in *Numen* vol.19. Brill, 1972.

Kvaerne, Per. *The Bon religion of Tibet.* London: Serindia Publications, 1995.

Lieblich, Amia & Tuval-Mashiach, Rivka & Zilber, Tamar. *Narrative research: reading, analyses and interpretation.* Thousands Oaks: Sage publications, 1998.

Lowenstein, Tom. *Boeddhisme. Filosofieën en meditatie, het pad naar spirituele verlichting, heilige plekken.* (Buddhism. Philosophy and meditation, the path towards spiritual enlightenment. Sacred places) Kerkdriel: Librero, 2003.

McKay, Alex (ed*.). The history of Tibet*, 1-3 vols. London and New York: RoutledgeCurzon, 2003.

Norbu, Dawa. 'The settlements: Participaton and Integration' in Bernstorff, Dagmar & Welck, Hubertus von (eds.). *The Tibetan diaspora, exile as challenge.* Delhi: Orient Longman Private Limited, 2003, p. 186-212.

Norbu, Namkhai. Drung, Deu and Bön. *Narrations, Symbolic languages and the Bon tradition in ancient Tibet.* Dharamsala: Library of Tibetan works and Archives, 1995.

Samuel, Geoffrey. *Civilized Shamans, Buddhism in Tibetan Societies.* London: Smithsonian Institution Press, 1993.

Snellgrove, David L. *Himalayan Pilgrimage.* Oxford: Bruno Cassirer LTD, 1961.

Snellgrove, David L. *The nine ways of the Bon.* London: Oxford University Press, 1967.

Skorupski, Tadeuz. *Tibetan G.yung-drung Bon Monastery in India in Tibet* Journal, vol. 11, no. 2 (Summer 1986), pp. 36-49.

Spradley, James. *The Ethnographic Interview.* New York: Holt, Reinhart & Winston, 1979.

Spradley, James. *Participant observation. New York*: Holt, Reinhart & Winston, 1980.

Tsomo, Karma Lekse. 'Tibetan nuns and nunneries' in Willis, Janice D (ed.). *Feminine Ground: Essays on woman and Tibet.* New York: Snow Lion Publications, 1987, p. 118- 134.

Tsomo, Karma Lekshe. 'Tibetan nuns: new roles and possibilities' in Bernstorff, Dagmar & Welck, Hubertus von (eds.). *The Tibetan diaspora, exile as challenge.* Delhi: Orient Longman Private Limited, 2003, p. 342 - 366.

Turner, Victor. *The ritual process: structure and anti-structure.* Chicago: Aldine Transaction, 1969.

Wester, Fred & Peters, Vincent. *Kwalitatieve Analyse, uitgangspunten en procedures.* (Qualitative analyses, principles and procedures) Bussum: Uitgeverij Coutinho, 2004.

Willis, Janice D. 'Tibetan Ani-s: The nun's life in Tibet' in Willis, Janice D (ed.). Feminine Ground: *Essays on woman and Tibet. New York:* Snow Lion Publications, 1987, p. 96-117.

Willis, Janice D (ed.). Feminine Ground: *Essays on woman and Tibet.* New York: Snow Lion Publications, 1987.

Other Sources

Velde, Paul J.C.L. van der. Notes of the lectures on Spirituality of Buddhism, May 9th 2007, Radboud Universiteit, Nijmegen.

Fieldwork notes of fieldwork in Dolanji, India August 2007 – October 2007.

Nuns Interviewed

Ani Sherap Sangmo
    Date of interview: 4 September 2007

Ani Tsundu Sangmo
    Date of interview: 4 September 2007

Ani Rinchen Sangmo
    Date of interview: 4 September 2007

Ani Metok Sangmo
    Date of interview: 5 September 2007

Ani Monlam Wangmo
    Date of interview: 6 September 2007

Ani Lobsang Wangmo
    Date of interview: 6 September 2007

Ani Tsewang Sherap
    Date of interview: 18 September 2007

Ani Yangzom Monlam
    Date of interview: 18 September 2007

Ani Tender Wangmo
    Date of interview: 19 September 2007

Ani Yangzo Dolma
    Date of interview: 19 September 2007

Ani Monlam Sangmo
    Datum interview: 20 September 2007

Ani Kunsel Wangmo
    Date of interview: 20 September 2007

Ani Tsering Lhamo
   Date of interview: 25 September 2007

Ani Tashi Tsomo
   Date of interview: September 2007

Ani Kunsang Lhamo
   Date of interview: 26 September 2007

Ani Namdak Lhamo
   Date of interview: 26 September 2007

Ani Tsultim Sangmo
   Date of interview: 27 September 2007

Ani Samten Wangmo
   Date of interview: 27 September 2007

Key persons interviewed

Geshe Latri Nyiama Dakpa Rinpoche: president of the Bon Childrens Home. Responsible for students studying outside Dolanji, member of the Yundrung Bon Monastic Center. Founder of the Bon Center in Vienna, Austria.

   Date of interview: 12 September 2007

Geshe Sonam: head and manager of the Guest House in Dolanji.

   Date of interview: 18 August 2007 and 19 September 2007

Geshe Shenphen Samdup: director Zang-Bod Documentation Center.

   Date of interview: 20 August 2007

His Holiness Menri Trizin Lungtok Tenpai Nyima: spiritual leader of the Bon and 33rd abbot of the Menri Monastery.

   Date of interview: 1 September 2007

Geshe Congtul Rinpoche: secretary-general of the Yundrung Bon Monastic Center, founder of the Bon Community Germany, founder of the Bon Ling Center in the USA, president of the Bon Cultural Center in Mongolia and India, president of the Friends of the Bon in Poland.

   Date of interview: 6 October 2007

Menri Lopan Rinpoche: head of the Geshe Training at Menri Monastery, Dolanji.

   Date of interview: 14 and 15 October 2007

Geshe Lhasay Tenzin: employed at the Yundrung Bon Monastic Center, in charge of the contacts between the center and the office of His Holiness.

   Date of interview: 20 October 2007

Geshe Tenzin Gelo: in charge of and supervisor of several building projects, in charge of the farm and treasurer of the Yundrung Bon Monastic Center.

   Date of interview: 20 October 2007